D0195046

Motherhood is this kind of honest gathering in book form. Through candid, poignant essays, this book pulls back the curtain of picture-perfect mothering and puts words to our raw feelings. A beautiful compilation of trusted voices articulates what we know our mama hearts are feeling but often don't know how to express. These sudden friends remind us of the beauty mothering brings to our lives, no matter how big the mess."

—ALEXANDRA KUYKENDALL, author of *Loving My Actual Life* and *The Artist's Daughter* and cohost of *The Open Door Sisterhood* podcast and retreat

"*The Magic of Motherhood* is a breath of fresh air for every mom who needs to be reminded that our journeys overlap in unexpected and yet predictable ways. When you need to regain a sense of equilibrium, this is the book that will bring you back to life."

—MANDY ARIOTO, president and CEO of MOPS International

"Motherhood is truly one of the best yet hardest jobs ever created. You are a personal assistant, a chef, a cheerleader, a therapist, and a chauffeur all rolled into one person. And there are days when the whole thing can feel like a giant pyramid scheme you were talked into by well-meaning friends who just wanted you to never sleep again. That's why I love the essays in *The Magic of Motherhood*. As we walk the road of motherhood, I think the questions on our minds are 'Am I doing this right?' and 'Does everyone feel this way sometimes?' As you turn the pages of this book, you'll realize the answer to both of these questions is *YES*. You will laugh and cry and alternately want to hug your kids a little tighter—and then send them off to play so you can read a few more pages!"

—MELANIE SHANKLE, *New York Times* bestselling author of *Sparkly Green Earrings*

"I laughed and cried through this entire book. Mothering is the most difficult adventure I've ever been on and one of the most rewarding ones as well. This book is full of stories that could have been written by every mother I know. You see, although mothering can feel lonely at times, this book is proof that we are all in this together. Us mamas need to stick together, and this book is proof that we all have the same issues, struggles, and love in us as everyone else."

—JAMIE IVEY, author and host of *The Happy Hour* podcast

"Moms don't want one more thing to do. We need more reminders that all those things we do matter. This book is that reminder. Let yourself sink into it, preferably while sinking into a bath (even if it does resemble the inside of a Toys"R"Us), and let these stories do their work—reminding you that what you do matters, every exhausting, seemingly invisible, and unbelievably hard and beautiful moment."

—LISA-JO BAKER, author of *Surprised by Motherhood* and community manager for (in)courage

PRESENTED TO:

____

FROM:

____

DATE:

____

The Magic of Motherhood

THE GOOD STUFF, THE HARD STUFF, AND EVERYTHING IN BETWEEN

ASHLEE GADD

AND THE WRITERS OF COFFEE + CRUMBS

ZONDERVAN®

ZONDERVAN

The Magic of Motherhood

This title is also available as a Zondervan e-book.

This title is also available as a Zondervan audio book.

Requests for information should be addressed to:

Zondervan, 3900 Sparks Dr. SE, Grand Rapids, Michigan 49546

Interior photography credits: Ashlee Gadd and N'Tima Preusser. Used with permission.
Artwork on pages 184–185 courtesy of Patti Murphy. Used with permission.

ISBN 978-0-3100-8460-0

Published in association with Creative Trust Literary Group, LLC, 210 Jamestown Park, Suite 200, Brentwood, Tennessee 37027, www.creativetrust.com.

Interior design: Lori Lynch

Printed in China

17 18 19 20 21 TIMS 10 9 8 7 6 5 4 3 2

CONTENTS

CONTENTS

INTRODUCTION

On May 7, 2012, a nurse placed a fresh seven-pound baby on my chest, and a wave fell over my body like fog cascading down a mountain. In that moment, we were all alone, even though there were six other people in the room.

Nothing could have prepared me for that love, for the raw emotion that enveloped every fiber of my being. Nothing could have prepared me for the daily sacrifice, for the way my body and soul would change time and time again, or for the challenges I would face in my marriage and friendships now that I was a mother.

As I dove headfirst into my new role, I quickly realized that I needed more than just sleep training books and a few lasagnas in the freezer. *Much* more.

I needed to know that I wasn't alone in this.

I needed encouragement and reassurance on the days when I felt invisible. I needed someone to look me in the eye and say, "I see you. You're a good mom."

Which is exactly how I want to start this book, so let me say that again:

INTRODUCTION

I see you. You're a good mom.

This is the book I wish I had received as a new mother. These pages are not full of suggestions or instructions (which is a good thing because we certainly aren't experts!). We aren't going to tell you how to parent, how to potty train, or how to do anything at all.

Rather than offering advice, we're offering ourselves. We're offering our hearts, our truths, our confessions, tiny epiphanies that came to us in the middle of the night. This is our collective memoir—stories that weave together the love, joy, and magnificent heartache of motherhood.

I like to think of this book as a quilt of sorts. We each show up with a few squares in our hands, and they all look and feel different. Some are soft with polka dots; others are bright with bold stripes. Some are frayed, and some have a few holes. Some squares are from days long forgotten, but as we began sorting through what we could bring to the table, we held them up and decided to try and salvage what remained. We believe with the right design and perfect thread, we can sew together these wild and beloved pieces to make something beautiful.

May this quilt serve as a marvelous reminder of our calling, of this holy work of motherhood, of our tattered stories and fairy tales, of where we have been and where we are going. May this quilt serve as a statement, a narrative, a piece of art woven together by one of the strongest threads God has given us here on earth—that of motherly love.

May it provide you comfort. May it always keep you warm.

Ashlee Gadd

1

A LETTER TO MY PRE-MOM SELF

by Ashlee Gadd

Oh, Momma. I see you over there in the diaper aisle of Target, stuffing your face with popcorn, an Icee tucked carefully between your arm and baby bump. You're staring at eight different kinds of baby wipes, trying to make life-impacting decisions for your unborn child: scented versus unscented, organic versus nonorganic, name brand versus generic.

Your brow furrows as you glance over your shoulder at the array of other choices staring at you—diaper bags, diaper pails, diaper rash creams. All the products sit neatly lined up on the shelves, mocking you.

"Pick me! Pick me!" they shout, trying to get your full attention in between bites of popcorn.

And what I really want to do is grab you by the shoulders and both yell and whisper sweetly at the same time: *It doesn't matter.* None of that *stuff* matters. It doesn't matter that you don't have a clue what you're doing or buying, because I'm going to let you in on a little secret: *nobody does.*

Nobody knows what they're doing bringing fresh new babies into the world. We're all clueless and equally terrified of doing everything wrong. We're all caught up in this newfound, captivating love, trying to figure it out one day at a time, one mistake at a time, one too-expensive Target trip at a time.

Nobody knows what they're doing bringing fresh new babies into the world.

I see the worry on your face, the anxiety in your heart, the ridiculous things you're Googling. It's okay. I know you're scared that life will never be the same, and you're right—it won't be. It will be both better and harder than the same, a paradoxical truth you won't fully understand until that squirmy, newborn baby is in your arms.

Although I have so much to tell you, so much gentle advice and encouragement to offer, I know that you will never fully comprehend any of this until you are living it. And yet, I cannot help myself . . . Here's what I want you to know:

You will be different. You will see parts of yourself that are unrecognizable, brought to the surface only by the sheer fact that another human is suddenly dependent on you for everything. You will be anxious; you will worry; you will feel overprotective like you've never felt before. You will simultaneously need space and not need space because all you want to do is be alone and also never leave your baby with anyone else. You will uncover a plethora of mom-related judgments that were hiding in your heart all along, and one by one, they will fall by the wayside as you realize just how difficult and messy and glorious this calling of motherhood actually is. You will learn to love fiercely and wildly without expectations, and for the first time in your entire life, your heart will default to selflessness—a part of you that always existed but was buried deep down inside—waiting for this moment, this change, this baby, this occasion to rise.

Your body will be different. Your body grew and sustained a human being, and those stretch marks on your belly are the well-earned badge of a warrior. It will take time to feel like yourself again, but one day you will look in the mirror with a newfound appreciation for all your body has done. You'll learn to do a myriad of tasks with a baby strapped to your chest, and just when you think you can't possibly get up one more time to rock him to sleep, you will. Motherhood will push your body to new limits, to new heights, to new possibilities. Above all else, your body will become a home for your children—your lap will become a place of security, your chest a place of warmth, your arms a place of assurance. Every inch of you will be used to care for these children, and though it's completely and utterly exhausting on most days, this superhero stamina is still a miracle worth noticing.

Your marriage will be different. You and your spouse will see each other with a whole new set of eyes, a brand-new microscope on each other's triumphs and failures. One of you will be "too carefree" and one of you will be "too careful." You will learn to meet in the middle . . . eventually. Regardless of where you disagree, no one in the world will love that baby more than the two of you, and that's an unbreakable bond you'll share for the rest of your lives. In the beginning, your date nights will be sparse. Your sex life will be slow. Be patient, be patient, be patient. You'll be tempted to keep score of everything: the number of times you were up in the middle of the night, the number of diapers you changed, who did the dishes last, whose job is harder. Listen to me carefully, Momma: *score-keeping has no place in your marriage.* The best thing you can do for yourself and for each other is to say "thank you" and "I love you" as much as possible. Be grateful. Be appreciative. Offer each other grace upon grace upon grace. You've never needed it this much.

Your house will be different. You will often feel overwhelmed by the mess, the piles of dishes, the sticky surfaces and crumbs. When you finally get around to cleaning, it lasts only a few hours, which makes you want to cry a little. But one day there will be a trail of Cheerios on the floor marking where your baby has been and what he has seen, and you'll realize that those Cheerios make your house feel more like a home than any fresh flower arrangement ever could, and that epiphany will make you smile. One day your toddler will run down the hallway in his footie pajamas, and you will want to capture that sound in a bottle for all of eternity because there is no better sound to wake up to (excluding the coffeemaker). Your house will be messier and

YOU WILL
LEARN TO
love FIERCELY
AND WILDLY
WITHOUT
EXPECTATIONS.

more chaotic, but you will love it a hundred times more because it has never felt more like *home*.

Your entire life will be different. Every single day, you will wake up with the responsibility and privilege of loving a child beyond measure. This will affect every decision you make, every thought you have, every fiber of your very existence. You will slowly learn to let go of control and expectations, a process you will practice every day for the rest of your life as a parent. You will start to see the world as a *mother*—you will see love and God and humanity through new eyes that will change you and mold you and make you more aware of how small you are and how big God is.

A void will be fulfilled that you didn't even know existed. Can you remember the first time you saw a sunrise? The first time your toes felt sand? The first time you tasted chocolate? Probably not. You were too young to remember. Five minutes before those experiences happened, you were cruising right along, thinking life was great as is. But then you saw that stunning orange sunrise and felt that warm sand between your toes and tasted that delicious piece of chocolate—and you knew. You knew that life had just become infinitely better because you experienced *magic*.

Motherhood is kind of like that, only a million times better.

So keep on shoppin', Momma. And remember what I said about the baby wipes: *that stuff doesn't matter.*

2

IN DEFENSE OF MOM JEANS

by Callie R. Feyen

It is 2004, and I am in a pizzeria in Washington, DC, with my husband, Jesse. I'm wearing black heels, a black tank top, and a pair of J.Crew jeans. These jeans are the best jeans I've ever owned. They sit on my hips perfectly, and I never have to pull them up or shift when I stand. They look spectacular with heels or flip-flops. They're my playful jeans, my brave jeans, my comfy jeans.

This restaurant is notoriously loud because it's small, but this is a family restaurant. I don't mind the noise. Actually, I swoon over it—the moms and dads spooning jarred baby food into the mouths of cherub babes as they kick happily.

"Do you think we'll do stuff like this when we have kids?" I ask Jesse, eyeing the families surrounding us.

"Eat pizza?" he says, putting another slice on my plate.

"You know, stroll to the neighborhood joint with our babies in tow."

"How many are we having?" Jesse says, mid-chew.

"I could have a lot," I say. "I think we could adopt too." I pour more wine into our glasses. "I mean, I teach middle school. How hard can motherhood be?"

More than ten years later, I'm at that same restaurant with Jesse; our two girls, Hadley and Harper; my brother and sister-in-law; their two kids, Mabel and Gus; and two more friends—girls in their early twenties. The place is still loud, and the volume makes us consider whether we should wait the forty-five minutes to be seated.

My brother, whose two-year-old is climbing all over his six-foot frame of a body, suggests we order and eat at their hotel. My sister-in-law, who holds Gus while he roots up and down her arm, thinks that's a good idea. I look at Hadley and Harper. They're nodding enthusiastically at their uncle's suggestion.

We order, and Jesse offers to wait for the pizzas so the younger kiddos can go home. Hadley and Harper stay with us, as do the two college girls.

One of them pulls out her phone and shows my girls this app that zombifies their faces. Hadley and Harper love it. She hands

them her phone (a rookie move, I think) and stands. "I could totally be a mom," she says.

We are standing inches away from where Jesse and I shared a pizza while I declared I could "totally" have lots of kids plus adopt because "I'm a middle school teacher, so how hard can it be?" I wince at the words I said years ago.

"Look," she continues, "I'm even wearing mom jeans. I totally *look* like a mom."

I look at my jeans. The college girl is wearing better jeans than I am. Acknowledging this and her hopeful confidence in becoming a mother makes me think of those J.Crew jeans and the girl who used to wear them.

The jeans came with me when I had to get a D&C because the baby I thought I was carrying was no longer. I folded them neatly and slid them in the plastic bag a nurse handed me when I walked into the hospital. "You'll get it all back when it's over," she said. *Not all of it*, I thought, standing in my bare feet and a surgical gown.

I would get pregnant again, and it would be a while before I'd wear the jeans, though I slipped them on and found they fit rather nicely the afternoon of Hadley's first birthday. That afternoon I'd been struggling to get her down for a nap.

My plan had been to take a shower during her nap, then bake Hadley's first birthday cake. Instead, we went to a bookstore and split a cinnamon scone. Hadley fell asleep in the stroller, so I bought a book and sat on a bench outside, reading while she slept. I crossed a leg and played with the hem of my jeans, happy to have a piece of my past on me the day my blue-eyed baby turned one.

Another time, the jeans came with me to the ER. Jesse and I were up all night with Harper, who'd just turned one, and had some sort of monster fever. And then she didn't. Within minutes, Harper's temperature went from the hundreds to below ninety. She was sitting on the bed between Jesse and me, and then she bowed forward, her head slamming into the mattress. Jesse scooped her up and took her to the ER.

I sat at our kitchen table, waiting for the phone to ring. When it did, and Jesse told me they were prepping Harper for a spinal tap, I grabbed Hadley from the crib and ran out the door. I was already wearing the jeans.

They say mothers can tell the difference in their children's cries: hungry versus tired and all that. I never could. Walking into the ER, though, Harper's cry is all I heard. I heard it above the sirens on the ambulances pulling in. I heard it above the TVs. I heard it above the receptionist requiring I check in.

She was on her back when I saw her, lying on a hospital bed. I rolled a chair so I could get closer to her, and my jeans (which were like Kleenex at the knees) ripped.

"Uh-oh, Mama," Harper said. She'd just learned to say *Mama* a few days ago.

"Uh-oh," I said back, nervously twiddling the hanging thread from the hole in my jeans.

Harper pointed to my knees. I grabbed her finger, and the thread broke free.

"Uh-oh," we said together over and over, like a psalm, holding a remnant of what was once whole.

I'm not sure that *whole* is the name of the game in motherhood. Motherhood means giving life, letting that life grow and be and become. When I bought my jeans, they had no label. They weren't skinnies, or boyfriend, date-night, or flare jeans. There were no expectations, and that was the magic: I could be whatever I wanted to be in them, and they'd go with me. They were the mother of all jeans.

The last time I remember wearing them was on our eleventh

anniversary. I'd made pot roast and a baguette. Jesse came home with cupcakes and champagne. When the girls had gone to bed, he handed me a present: a subscription to *Writer's Digest*, a notebook, and a pack of pens. "For all your stories," he said, then pulled out a pamphlet for a course called "Writing Motherhood" at a local writing center.

"It's on Tuesday at 10:00 a.m.," I said, giving the pamphlet back to him. "I can't do this."

"We'll get a babysitter," he said. He handed the pamphlet back to me. "You are always a mother. You are not *only* a mother."

The jeans stopped working after that. I think the button at the waist fell off, or maybe the hem ripped. I can't remember, but I've never had a pair like those jeans since. It's hard to find something that shows off all the complexities of who we are. It takes more than clothing.

Recently, I was in Hadley's classroom for a book club. "Do you have a favorite part?" I asked. "How about a part that confused you?" I watched Hadley carefully because I didn't want to embarrass her, but Hadley had a huge smile on her face.

"Mama," she whispered, "Tell them what you do! Tell them what you are!"

I didn't know what to say, but Hadley answered for me.

"My mom's a writer!" She exclaimed, her eyes wide. "She's a teacher too!"

"And I'm your mom," I said, ruffling her hair.

"Well, yeah," Hadley said, rolling her eyes. "They know that."

+ + +

The pizza is here, so we turn and walk toward the door. I take another look at the table Jesse and I sat at more than a decade ago, and remember what I said and all that has passed. I take another look at the jeans of the college girl who's holding Harper's hand as they walk outside. I think she's right: she can totally be a mom. And she's wearing the perfect jeans.

3

THE THINGS THAT COME AROUND AGAIN

by Elena Krause

The fire always starts in front of my house, a single spark in the branches hanging over our porch. It consumes the whole canopy and jumps to the next one in a split second, roaring down the block until all the neighbors' yards are ablaze with fall colors. It's fast. I hardly ever catch that first little flash in time—but even if I could, I wouldn't be able to stop it.

When I notice it's begun, I like to go out and sit on my front steps, right under the burning trees. They crackle quietly as the wind moves them and they drop their bright orange leaves like glowing embers onto my lawn. I scoop up these ashes in garbage bags and throw them into the alley to be carried away and burned again. This fire, as fires do, burns only until it has nothing left to eat or until winter comes and the snow puts it out.

It's a bittersweet process, the changing of the seasons. The switch itself is beautiful—the fire in the trees, the long shadows on the ground, the harvest sunsets, the cool air on sunburned skin. But I live on the Canadian prairies, and the start of winter also means the end of a lot of things I love. The lake freezes solid, and the lawn chairs are packed away into the back of the garage along with the grill and the baseball gloves. We pull the parkas out from under the stairs and watch the geese leave in flocks. Those who can afford it follow the birds. The rest of us head indoors.

That spark, that first orange leaf, always makes me feel sad. I tend to start missing things before they're gone. *At least,* I think to myself as I watch the burnt leaves fall, *summer will come around again.*

Because that is how seasons work. That's how almost everything works. Life is, after all, a very cyclical kind of thing.

It's 7:00 p.m. and I'm snuggled up in a rocking chair with my son under a green and yellow knitted baby blanket that used to belong to his dad. The fire is still burning outside the window. It fills the room with a warm amber light that shifts on the walls and plays on the pages of the book open in front of us.

I'VE ALWAYS THOUGHT OF NOSTALGIA AS KIND OF A SAD FEELING, BUT MAYBE IT'S MORE OF A *blessing*.

We've read this particular book every night for the past several months; it's one my mom read to me when I was his age. He calls it the bear book.

I have the bear book almost memorized by now, word for word, but tonight I paraphrase instead, pointing at the familiar characters. "Look," I say to him, "there's a big bear and a little bear. The little bear is afraid of the dark." I turn the page.

My son pushes away from me. "I read it myself," he announces. He scoots to the end of my knees and jumps off. Settling onto the floor at my feet, he cracks the book open once again; he starts at the beginning. He points to the little bear. "Little bear," he says. "Little bear afraid."

I feel something familiar, and I realize it's sadness—the same sadness I feel when I see the spark in the trees. It's the start of the end of something I love—only this is different. I can't smile and say to myself, *At least his childhood will come around again*. My son grins up at me from the floor. "Big bear," he says. "Big bear give little bear a hug. Little bear happy."

"Want to come back here and sit on my lap?" I ask, feeling a little desperate to have him near me.

"No," he says. "I read it myself." He's proud.

I nod. "Okay, buddy." And I realize this isn't the first spark at all; that happened almost two years ago when he smiled at me for the first time. He is a whole tree full of red leaves.

"You okay?" asks my husband when I come out of our son's room.

"Yes," I say in a helium voice. It feels like my brain is pushing against the backs of my eyes.

He raises his eyebrows.

I sit beside him on the couch and take a drink of his coffee without asking. "He wouldn't let me read his bedtime story tonight." There is silence; he's probably trying to understand why this would upset me so much. "I guess I just feel like motherhood is a lot of wishing away hard seasons and then realizing they're gone forever. It's trying to claw back through time because you didn't realize what you were actually wishing away. Like when he wasn't sleeping through the night? I just kept thinking, *Soon, he will. This will be over, and he'll sleep through the night.* And now I think, *That wasn't so bad. At least I got to snuggle him to sleep every night back then.* I sleep eight-hour nights and I want to go back to catnapping in forty-five-minute chunks just so my kid will fall asleep in my lap. This is ridiculous. Who *am* I?"

My husband gives me a hug because he knows better than to agree with me when I say I'm being ridiculous. I am ridiculous a lot of the time.

I wander out onto the porch to sit under the fire and reflect. Despite the flaming leaves above me, the air is cold. *Stupid October.* Fall is not my favorite season.

Moms always use that word—*season*—when they talk about their children. *This season of life is temporary. We're in a tricky season, a fun season, a short season, a long season.*

But that word feels wrong because seasons are circular, and childhood is a line. When this tree I'm sitting under has dropped all of its leaves, it'll shiver for a few months, and then it'll sprout new ones. It gets to start over. If we didn't savor the warmer months enough, we can take solace in the fact that we'll get another chance—but when my son has sat on my lap for the last time, that'll be it. It won't come around again.

I rest my chin in my hand and frown at the fire. It's burning so fast, and I can't stop it.

+ + +

I'm on the front steps again, only it's spring now and the trees are starting to bud. The breeze is warming up, and the birds are back.

Every fall, when I'm mourning the loss of summer, I forget about this part—the part where new things grow and turn the neighborhood bright green. Summer is ahead instead of behind, and there are things to look forward to instead of things to miss.

And there's excitement in knowing what's coming next. The days get longer and warmer, the birds lay their eggs down by the water, and the kids play in the streets again. The apple tree in the backyard turns bright white with blossoms, and you look down the street and think, *Was it this green last year? I don't think it's ever been this green before.*

You don't get to live the last summer over again, but you remember it because there are bits of it that still exist in this one. The heat from the sun on your face, a warm breeze, even the grating itch of mosquito bites on your bare legs. I've always thought of nostalgia as kind of a sad feeling, like a longing for what was but isn't anymore. But maybe it's more of a blessing. It's bits of the past that have stuck around and hang in the air of the present.

My son is playing in front of me on the grass, driving little toy trucks across the lawn. He doesn't fall asleep on me anymore, but he tells me he loves me, and he means it. The first time he did that, it was like spring, like a little green bud in the place of a leaf that had withered up and fallen down. It was the start of something new, but it was a familiar new thing.

Someday these leaves will burn up and he'll be a kid who goes to school, and I'll miss him—but he'll be okay. It will be another new beginning, another spring. Someday he won't live in my house anymore, but maybe he'll meet someone special and start a family. And then maybe, the moment he lays eyes on his own baby, he'll catch a glimpse into how I feel about him. That will be another spring.

Each new thing will have traces of the old things. I picture looking my son in the eyes when he's twenty-five and recognizing the toddler who once snuggled into me so I could read to him from the bear book.

I guess childhood only looks like a straight line when you're close to it, but when you pull back far enough, you see that it's cyclical too. The leaves falling from the tree are beautiful, but they're not the tree. Each new season and year brings its own beauty.

4

ASKING FOR HELP

by Lesley Miller

There came a moment in my second pregnancy when people at the grocery store started wincing as soon as I walked through the double doors. Unfortunately, this moment did not come at the nine-month-and-three-days mark, or even at the eight-month mark. This was one of those classic second pregnancies where I started getting pudgy about two days after conception. At seven months along strangers routinely asked if I was having twins, and everyone seemed to ask, "Any day now?"

Apparently people still have not learned how to just nicely say, "You are glowing, and I am so happy for your growing family." But that's another conversation for another day.

On one particular afternoon in the Trader Joe's checkout aisle, as my almost-two-year-old was pulling gum and candy off the shelves, I made a wonderful mistake. When the bagger asked if I wanted help to the car, words came out of my mouth that never had before.

"Yeahhh," I said hesitantly, followed by something like, "but are you sure?"

The guy looked at me with great concern, as if my water might break any moment and a child could burst forth if he didn't help. Then he said, "Absolutely. I'd love a chance to get outside."

I'm not sure why, but until that moment I believed that accepting help to the car was a privilege reserved for those truly in need. The blind. The elderly. Bomb victims. I was strong and my legs worked fine. Never mind that I had a squirming two-year-old rifling through the bags. Never mind that my belly was bigger than Africa. Never mind that it was almost a hundred degrees in their crowded, horrible, terrifying parking lot where impatient people lose their minds waiting for the slow pregnant lady to load up her toddler, eggs, and twelve varieties of ice cream.

I guess . . . I suppose . . . some help might be nice. Just today.

It felt odd to watch someone else push my cart to the car, and it was even weirder to have him stack my groceries in the trunk with no expectation for a tip. I think he asked when the baby was due, and I told him probably never. When I thanked him—and I was so thankful—he said it was his pleasure.

As I drove home that day, I couldn't stop thinking about how easy it all felt. I didn't even have to waddle the cart back to the stack while my little one sat in a hot car. By the time I pulled into my driveway, I was wondering why the checkout boy hadn't offered to come home and carry those groceries into my kitchen. Receiving that offer of help felt so good—so necessary.

Why had I said no to help my entire life?

To no one's surprise, I delivered a huge, almost ten-pound baby boy later that summer. Technically, he was the combined weight of many twin births, so I suppose all those strangers' comments were accurate. Even though I'm not pregnant anymore (and I'm not blind or using crutches either), I've been enthusiastically accepting help to my car every time we visit a grocery store. When it comes to receiving help, I've replaced "Are you sure?" with "Absolutely. Yes." And now, after a rather embarrassing incident involving one of my children throwing an entire carton of blueberries in the parking lot, I've taken an even bigger step. If no one offers to help me, I often ask.

Receiving that offer of help felt so good—so necessary. Why had I said no to help my entire life?

This revolution has gone beyond the grocery store. In the newborn days, when I was sleep deprived and angry, I asked my mom to watch the kids so I could be alone for a few hours to take care of myself. When my son wasn't talking very much at eighteen months, I called a speech therapist for a free evaluation. When my kids both woke up vomiting, I texted my neighbors and asked them to bring over provisions like applesauce, Pedialyte, and carpet cleaner. These requests may sound like no-brainers to some, but they were big, humbling moments for me. I like feeling strong, and I take pride in my independence. I don't usually ask for help, even when I'm desperate. And I don't think I'm alone in this.

Are you feeling desperate today?

There's something you need to know. You are not weak if you need backup. You aren't needy if you ask your husband to take a late-night diaper change. You are not lazy if you ask grandparents to watch the kids sometimes, or if you hire a housecleaner because you barely have time to bathe yourself, let alone scrub the tile. Mothers—whether we stay at home, work from home, work full time or work overtime—are managing a whole lot of crazy. And sometimes we need help.

As I began recognizing my own needs, a very special thing happened: I also started noticing others' needs in a way I hadn't before. The more I've said yes to help, the better I've become at offering it to others. When my girlfriend's husband was out of town for the week, I offered to babysit her kids so she could go grocery shopping. When a woman from church mentioned a particularly long week at work, we dropped off takeout. A beautiful, natural give-and-take happens when we humbly let down our guard and help each other.

So start saying yes in the grocery store line. Start asking for a hand when yours are full. And please stop telling yourself you need to have it all together, because none of us do. Isn't that freeing?

There's still a lot about motherhood I haven't figured out, but I do know this: we cannot journey alone.

A BEAUTIFUL, NATURAL, GIVE AND TAKE HAPPENS WHEN WE *humbly* LET DOWN OUR GUARD AND HELP EACH OTHER.

5

THE WOMAN IN THE HALL

by April Hoss

There is a remarkable photograph on the dresser in our hallway. It lives in a frame I stopped liking three years ago. My son is in the picture. He is four days from his first birthday, dressed like Charlie Brown, and smiling at the camera. He is sitting on the lap of his mother. The first one. The one who gave him life.

I promised her we'd always keep that picture up. I think that's when she believed the other promises I'd made. The ones about always loving her son and protecting her son, and raising him with such blurred love no one would believe he was adopted.

Those promises have been easiest to keep. The picture is proving to be the challenge.

+ + +

My voice rang upbeat and agreeable when the social worker called me to say my son's birth mom wanted to restart visitations. He had been home only a week and was still legally considered a foster child in our care, so there wasn't a whole lot more I could do other than say, "Yes ma'am," and ask when and where.

But inside, I was screaming. I was terrified.

That we'd had him only seven days, that we'd not conceived him or birthed him, that under a microscope it would look like he wasn't ours: those were details.

He was our son from the second we knew he existed. Actually, for much longer than that. God chose this boy to be our very own before any of us existed. But now I had to show up to an office complex to take my child to a woman who wanted him too.

I've never prayed with such fervor.

Then she walked in, his biological mother. And with a few steps toward me, in the two seconds our eyes met and I saw her smile, I felt something like love at first sight.

It could have been that she limped a little, or that she'd obviously tried to dress up. It might have been that her eyes are identical to my boy's. She was his mother. And she was a child. Just like that, I wanted to adopt her too.

We talked for hours at that first visit. She held our sleeping baby in the rocking chair, and I leaned forward against the kidney-shaped kids' table and asked question after question. She told me about her life and the four different high schools she'd been to, how she had grown up in foster care and had never gotten a family. She described the fight at the group home when she lost her earlobes.

> **When friends and extended family suggested she do the smart thing and terminate her pregnancy, she said no.**

And she told me that when friends and extended family suggested she do the smart thing and terminate her pregnancy, she said no.

"They offered me, like, rides and stuff. You know, they thought I should just do an abortion or whatever. But I said no. I never been to church or anything but I know there's a Jesus and I know there's a God, and He told me I was supposed to have this baby. He told me it was gonna be a boy. That was before they did that computer test where they tell you what your baby is. I already knew he was a boy. God told me to have him."

I'm certain that's what she said for two reasons. First, I was so moved I wrote it down the moment I got home. I wanted to ensure I could tell my son someday. Second, I didn't need to write it down. I will never forget sitting in that room, with the afternoon light highlighting all the grime on the county-owned toys, and listening to a teenage girl with no money and no resources and no family and no help tell me she chose to let my son live because Jesus told her that was the plan.

That was it for me. A turning point if there ever was one. He was mine and she was mine and we could all make this work.

The only question: how?

My husband and I wanted some connection to her, a relationship of some kind. Maybe letters, or pictures e-mailed back and forth, or a Christmastime visit every year. The details were murky and ever changing, but one thing was certain: we didn't want to lose her.

The social workers handling our case had different ideas. They discouraged an ongoing relationship, elevating positive

sayings like "fresh start," and "when he's ready," and "a new beginning."

Not a lot of *I know there's a Jesus* and *I know there's a God* coming from their end. My son's mom was a lost cause in the annals of their dull green file folders. With one final visit scheduled, I knew time really was running out.

So my mom and I did what we do—we planned a party. We were already elbow deep in a Peanuts-themed first birthday party for Ridley when we learned his birth mom had never had a birthday party of her own. Not once. No fifth birthday at Chuck E. Cheese, no slumber parties at ten, no sweet sixteen. On her actual eighteenth birthday I got a phone call saying her son had been chosen for me. How's that for a present?

Ridley and his birth mom are one day shy from sharing half birthdays. What's one day? I told the social workers that my mom and I would like to throw Ridley's mom her very first birthday party to celebrate his first birthday. "Since she gave him life, it only makes sense to celebrate hers. He wouldn't be here without her," I explained.

Their answer: "Yeah, that will be a good chance to say good-bye."

There will come a moment when Ridley looks at the picture in the hall and asks me to tell him about that day. The day me and his grandma threw a party for his mom. The first one. This is what I'll say:

It was hard for Mama M to get there. She was living with a cousin while she waited for her little studio to be ready. The state was moving her foster services into a self-reliant apartment group, and on the day of the party she was in between homes. It was difficult to find someone to bring her to you; the party was two hours away, a location chosen by well-meaning social workers who really believed distance was the very best thing.

I told Mama M we would be taking pictures at a real photography studio. It was the kind of place that most people scoff at, the cheesy kind at the mall, but she'd never had a professional photo taken, and she was thrilled. And nervous. Boy, she was nervous. That was my favorite thing about her. Despite the total chaos and large doses of horror in her life, she was still, always, a teenage girl who wanted to look cute in front of the camera.

Finally, we spotted her, Grandma and I. Mama M had found a way. She was dressed in yellow and black, an homage to your upcoming, extravagant Peanuts party. She confessed she'd stayed up till 3:00 a.m. figuring out what to wear. She wanted the yellow to be just right, and she only had one pair of black pants, and while she hated what she'd landed on (like I said, a teenager through and through), she looked great.

I don't think anyone trustworthy ever told her she was beautiful. She was. Like a distant cousin of both Snow White and the Girl with the Dragon Tattoo. I wish I had told her that day, as she straightened her shirt before pictures, *Hey M, you look beautiful*. Add that to my list of regrets.

You and your mama took pictures, and then she surprised me and wanted some with me too. The photographer, nice but a teensy bit dense, said something like, "Is this a two-mommy situation?" Your grandma, quick on the draw, said, "This is a birthday situation." There were no more questions.

I like those pictures of the three of us: me, you, and M. It looks just exactly like it felt. Not awkward, not tense, no anger under the surface. A tired baby and an excited teenager and a twenty-nine-year-old desperately trying to make sure everyone was okay.

"She thinks of you like a sister," your social worker said more than once. I guess I should have asked, "Does she want to be my kid?"

After the photos, Mama M and Gram put you in the stroller and walked to the restaurant while the social worker and I paid for the photos and frames. We got your first mama a big collage, plus some loose pictures and a key chain with a picture of you on both sides. Her favorite was the one of you in the blue cloth diaper because she was always tickled by your chubby thighs. Nothing made her laugh like that, like you.

Before lunch the three of you rode the little mall train, and Mama M told Gram it was her first time on a real train. Gram tried not to cry, and Mama M waved at all the people. Gram can't help but chuckle when she describes how some shoppers hesitated a second before waving back at the exuberant teenage girl on the little red train.

GOD SPOKE AND

YOU ANSWERED,

AND BECAUSE

OF THAT A

LITTLE BOY

breathes.

At lunch we told M to order whatever she wanted, so there were Cokes and spring rolls and pizza and artichoke dip. You gave her two birthday presents: a Peanuts coffee mug filled with candy so she could have a piece of your party; and dragonfly earrings, big and gold and very sparkly. You brought a dragonfly toy to all your visits; it was your favorite toy at the time. The two of you played with it together and I noticed, though her earlobes were gone, she'd gotten her ears pierced just the same. It took me weeks to find gold dragonfly earrings. It was worth the hunt.

"I can wear these every day," she said. She put them on that instant.

I swallowed hard. I had something to say. "M, I hope you know you saved his life." She looked up at me, confused. "Remember when you told me how some people in your life suggested an abortion and God told you not to have it done? Remember how we kind of talked about that at our first visit?"

I treaded lightly here, now wondering if she remembered that conversation or didn't want me to mention it in front of my mom.

She smiled though. I said, "He is not turning one because of me." You squawked for more chocolate cake and flashed us a two-tooth grin. "He gets to have birthdays because of you, M. When he graduates high school and goes to college and gets married and has his own kids, that's all because of you." Here I realized how awkward I sounded and how impossible it was to actually thank someone for not killing my child while he still resided in her womb. They don't make cards for that moment. Consulting the Internet is of little help. I tried to land the plane.

"I am so thankful to you, M. Thank you for giving him life. For being brave enough to listen to God. Someday he is going to want to thank you too."

She gave me, then the social worker, a quizzical look. "I didn't save his life," she said. The social worker, a woman who had known M since she was a little girl taken in by CPS, nodded her head. She knew before I did what M was trying to say.

"Ridley was your knight in shining armor, wasn't he?"

Your first mama laughed a little. "Yeah. A lot of crazy stuff happened to me. I survived because of him. He saved me."

I don't remember much after she said that. I know Gram and I stopped at a baby store because you needed new shoes. I know M had trouble getting a ride home and ended up leaving with a social worker.

I know she carried you to your big blue stroller and she buckled you in. She said, "I love you, baby," and kissed your head, and right after that you fell asleep.

I hugged her. I told her happy birthday. I watched her walk away.

Dad and I put the picture in the hall that night. It sits closest to your door, just outside in fact. I think of M all the time and see her every day. I pray when we have this conversation I can tell you she's okay. She found her way.

If there comes a day that I see her again and she asks what happened to the pictures we took that day, I will say this: "M, I love you. You're beautiful. I hope you know that by now, and I hope you learned early that has little to do with hair and eyeliners and filters you can download for free. Wherever we go, you go, and not just the moment in a photograph locked in a silver frame. God spoke and you answered, and because of that, a little boy breathes. He lives, M. To us, forever, you were never just a picture in the hall."

6

WONDER WOMAN

by Anna Quinlan

When I grow up, I want to be Wonder Woman!" my five-year-old son exclaimed.

"Oh, really?" I asked, opting to hear him out before going anywhere near the daunting topic of gender identity. "And why's that?"

"Wonder Woman is the coolest superhero," he explained. "She doesn't even have any weapons. She just has her arms and her legs, and she *wonders* a lot."

And from the mouth of my very own babe, there it was: the true definition of supermom.

It couldn't have come at a better time. The supermom trope

had haunted me at every turn on my winding road of motherhood, and I was desperate to find shelter from its oppression.

When I was pregnant with my first son, I had a job that had been slowly crushing my soul. For many years of my relatively happy career, I had dreaded the moment I would have to decide whether to go the working-mom or the stay-at-home-mom route. But now that the decision was upon me, having a job I hated gave me the gift of an easy decision: I would gladly walk away and try my hand at home.

And it was great. We stenciled birds on the nursery wall. I read the sleep books, followed the steps, and my baby slept through the night. I made baby food. I breastfed him for ten months and didn't get mastitis once. I meal-planned and made dinner during the baby's afternoon nap. I carpooled to a moms group every Tuesday morning with my friend whose baby was just two months younger than mine. I was doing it. I was supermom.

Until I wasn't. My easy baby grew into a very strong-willed toddler, and another baby arrived when the first was just nineteen months old. The new baby got formula and store-bought baby food. He slept in a bassinet in our bedroom until his first birthday because he wouldn't sleep through the night. Afternoon phone calls to my husband became the norm.

"When are you coming home?" I begged. "Pick up dinner on your way."

The relief of unemployment wore off. I started to unravel. Supermom had left the building.

Eventually, I went back to work. I wore pencil skirts again. I scheduled pediatrician appointments during my lunch break. I

I STARTED TO UNRAVEL. *Supermom* HAD LEFT THE BUILDING.

made giant batches of chicken gumbo and Tex-Mex casserole on the weekends and stocked the freezer full of weeknight dinner options. I went to the gym after the kids were in bed and did some freelance writing after that. I was making it work. I was supermom 2.0.

But there were chinks in the armor, of course. My post-tax salary barely covered the child care it necessitated, and I wondered if I was selfish to be working outside the home while my kids were so young. I could never keep up with the paperwork that kept coming home from preschool—the permission slips and homework and reading lists and volunteer "opportunities." I suspected that I was the token delinquent mom, that the teachers were shaking their heads behind my back about how my pencil skirts belied my ineptness. My son proclaimed that pink was a "girl color" one day, and I chastised myself for personally failing to demonstrate that girls and boys can like any color of the rainbow, thank you very much. I was failing as a feminist. I was failing as a PTA member. I was failing as a mom.

If only I could develop better systems, I thought to myself again and again as I rifled through the various stacks of paper in every room of the house. *If only I had more help. If only my three-year-old would sleep through the night. If only my kids were quieter, less messy. If only I could get it all together. If only I could control everything. Surely then I would finally be supermom, once and for all.*

Except that's not how it works. While I was busy searching for secret weapons and aspiring for control, my five-year-old

was way ahead of me. *She doesn't have any weapons. Just her arms and her legs, and she wonders a lot.*

In my never-ending quest to equip myself with better tools and better systems, I had overlooked the fact that I had *myself*. Not just my arms and my legs, but my character, my sense of humor, my passion, and my bottomless love for my kids. In my desire for control, I had lost all sight of the value of curiosity, of *wondering*.

I was aiming far too low. I was aiming for order instead of wonder, mastery instead of stewardship, a certificate of achievement instead of an invitation for growth. I don't want to be supermom anymore. I want to be Wonder Woman.

I want to show my kids what it looks like to face the world unarmed and unafraid. I want to show them that the ability to stay curious is the greatest superpower of all. But like any feat of parenting, if I want these ideas to stick, I have to live them in my own life, both privately and publicly, because my kids are always watching. I have to embody Wonder Woman's ideals not just when I hope to teach my kids a lesson, but when I have a lesson to learn myself.

When my kids are defiant and I am frustrated, can I stay curious then? Will I rush to the Internet for a new method to squash the bad behavior, or will I be able to wonder at these little people with their very own minds and ideas? When they are angelic and I am tempted to congratulate myself for raising them so well, can I stay curious then? What will they see on my face when they look up at me: answers or wonder?

I hope they see a little spark of Wonder Woman in me. I hope they understand that supermom doesn't exist, because motherhood is far too fantastic to master. It is truly the stuff of a comic book galaxy far, far away: mysterious, scary, daunting, adventurous, filled with angels and demons, and never giving away what comes next.

But we are equipped for it. Not with the weapons of a hollow supermom character, but simply with ourselves and our wonder.

7

BEING THE VILLAGE

by Anna Jordan

"I'm pregnant," she said. "Like, probably four weeks along. Maybe a little more."

This particular memory is housed in one of the deepest, warmest parts of my heart. In my mind, the entire experience is encased in a rosy, golden hue: my brand-new baby daughter snuggled in the arms of my sweet friend, Corinne, who would soon have her own new baby. I remember the sunlight streaming in from the hospital window, the smile on her face. I'm sure there was some noise in the hallway. I know that my abdomen was aching with the fresh wound of my C-section. I think a tray of lunch and maybe even a dirty diaper cluttered the hospital bed, and crumpled blankets lay around my legs. But those images are all muted in my memory. Everything stopped the moment she said those words. She was going to have a baby. The baby we'd prayed for. The baby we'd wept for. The baby we had waited and waited to meet. That baby was coming.

Honestly, I had been worried about my friend visiting me in the hospital. She had spent two long, hard years trying to conceive her second child. After months of negative tests and two miscarriages, she worried—we all worried—that perhaps she would never conceive again. To add to the pain and complexity of it all, my third baby arrived unexpectedly. A surprise pregnancy that shocked us with joy and, frankly, quite a bit of stress. When I discovered I was pregnant, my older children were two

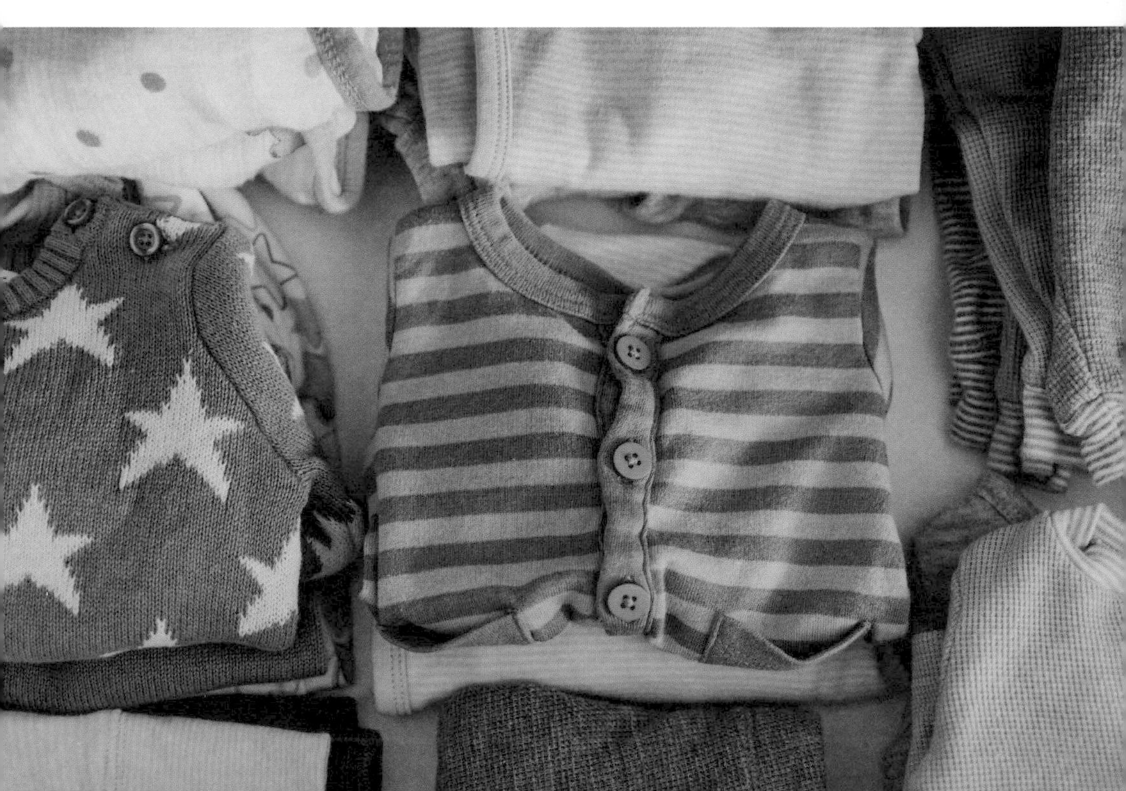

years old and ten months old. I hadn't even had time to think about a third baby, but she was on her way whether we liked it or not.

As my pregnancy progressed, my feelings of joy and excitement, and even fear and frustration, were comingled with guilt. I had what my friend so desperately wished for, and more often than not, I didn't feel particularly grateful for what I had. But she was a good friend, a steady friend, and we had nearly a decade of camaraderie under our belts. Still, I worried—until she said the phrase we'd all been longing to hear: "I'm pregnant."

The birth of my daughter is always going to be significant—she's my daughter—but her birth also coincides with another incredible joy: the joy of my friend.

We always talk about how it takes a village to raise a child. Baby showers and meal calendars are commonplace topics of pre-baby conversations. The people who love us gather round to help prepare for the new life. Before I became a mother, and then in my five years since joining the ranks of motherhood, I've been acutely aware of the benefits of having a village around me.

On New Year's Eve day last year, all three of my children had the stomach flu. My house was a disaster, covered in beach towels and barf bowls. The baby only wanted to be carried, and my older two wanted to lie head to foot on the couch to watch a movie but, of course, couldn't stand to share a blanket, let alone touch. Fighting, vomiting preschoolers, and a needy diarrhea baby are not anyone's idea of a rockin' New Year's Eve. There was no way any of us were making it to midnight. That afternoon, I was in the midst of what felt like the three hundredth load of laundry when I heard a light tap on my front door. One of my girlfriends was standing on the doorstep with a small box of dark chocolate peanut butter cups: "Hide these. They're just for you. Good luck!"

I almost cried. Her midday treat drop-off wasn't a big gesture, but it was just what I needed. She knew I was spending the day caring for three tiny people who needed me desperately, and she took the opportunity to care for me.

I suppose it's natural to think about all the ways I benefit from having a loving community around me. I've been consistently surprised by the generosity of my village and overwhelmed with the thankfulness I feel in being part of it.

When our oldest was placed with us, I only had a baby crib and one blanket. My husband and I thought we would have to wait longer for a baby, and since we were adopting through the foster system, we didn't know how old our child would be. It was hard to adequately anticipate our needs, so we were fully unprepared. While we were signing papers and finishing up the required foster parent training courses, my sweet girlfriends planned a baby shower for us, and to tide us over, my friend Megan brought over a giant bag of brand-new clothes. She popped by on the day we brought our son home, snapped our first photo as a family of three, and snuggled our new little boy while I waded through a pile of adorable clothes: sweatpants, onesies, sleepers. She had fully outfitted him.

One of my favorite items from Megan was a grey Henley onesie with navy blue trim and navy blue buttons. My son wore it only a few times before his chunky legs and barrel chest threatened to burst the seams, so I washed the onesie carefully, folded it, and placed it—along with the other too-small clothes—into a box and saved it. Two years later, my friend Caitlin had a baby boy, and I passed the box of my son's hand-me-downs on to her.

Well, wouldn't you know it, one year later another one of my girlfriends had a baby boy. Caitlin passed the clothes along to our friend Leah and her new little guy. These onesies were surprisingly durable, for the most part. We'd lost a couple to blowouts and spit-up, but that grey Henley was holding strong.

Leah's son is now nearly two, and just a few months ago she washed and folded all her son's hand-me-downs and put them in a bag for Megan and *her* new baby boy. Some of the clothes Megan had bought for me nearly five years ago had come full circle.

We all felt teary to see Megan's little boy in that durable Henley. It's more than just a faded grey onesie with three blue buttons; it's a love letter from all of us, the mothers who have the privilege of loving him. It's a visual reminder of the continued blessing of friendship and the ways we've supported and cared for each of our babies over the years. Because we haven't just passed a onesie around, *Sisterhood of the Traveling*

Pants–style. The clothes are just one thread in the larger fabric of our relationship.

Between pregnancies, childbirths, baby showers, and birthday parties, we do the hard work of mothering side by side. We've lamented potty training woes and shared tips on how to discipline a sassy threenager. We've passed around Pack 'n Plays and baby bassinets along with mastitis-prevention tips and recipes for lactation cookies.

Because of my bonds of friendship, my children have a rich extended family of close friends. They're not even in elementary school yet and they regularly refer to their "people." My children love and fight with these friends like siblings, and as a result, we're all unpacking a deeper understanding of forgiveness and conflict resolution. Before motherhood, I had no idea how dear the babies of my friends would be to me, and I didn't realize I would feel the growth and development of my girlfriends' children so deeply. It turns out, one of the most wonderful joys of motherhood is the other mothers.

Last week Megan passed along that Henley to Corinne. She gave birth to a beautiful baby boy, and I can't wait to watch him grow—to be part of his village.

8

THE HIDDEN GIFT

by Ashlee Gadd

"Everett! Go get your socks! We're leaving!" I yell.

We're running late, surprise, surprise. Six months into life with two kids, you'd think I'd have this down by now.

Why didn't I get our stuff ready last night? After all, I know what the morning holds: a halfhearted attempt at a decent shower while the baby screams bloody murder, a nursing session, a spit-up session, a change of clothes for both of us, a diaper blowout, Cheerios spilled on the couch, and one cup of lukewarm coffee. This chaos is nothing if not predictable.

Last night I chose Netflix over packing the diaper bag, which is why I'm standing in the kitchen with a baby on my hip, washing grapes in the sink and trying to remember where I put my car keys.

My hands fly through the motions—grapes in the lunch box, add an ice pack, dip the baby ever so slightly while I put detergent in the dishwasher, click start, flip the TV off, slip phone into my back pocket. I throw the diaper bag over my shoulder and glance at the microwave clock. We should have left ten minutes ago.

I never thought of myself as "strong" until I had children.

Let's call it what it is: this stage of mothering is incredibly physical. It's hard on my body to carry these kids around all day, lifting them in and out of car seats, in and out of bathtubs, on and off high chairs and booster seats and potties. I never thought of myself as "strong" until I had children. I continue to be amazed at my ability to carry a sleeping child (along with five grocery bags, a purse, and a water bottle) into the house from the car in one swift motion. Besides, who needs the gym when you can lift a double stroller into the trunk of a car with a baby strapped to your chest? *I am mother; hear me roar.*

On my best days, I feel like I was built for this. On my worst days, I feel like an elderly woman with tender feet and a sore back. Sometimes around 5:00 p.m. you can find me lying facedown on the floor, begging my three-year-old to roll his monster trucks up and down my spine. It pales in comparison to a real massage, but I'll take what I can get.

I often find myself staring into space, dreaming of what it will be like when my kids can put on their own shoes. Better yet: I dream of the day when I will no longer be fully knowledgeable about their bowel movements.

In my most exhausted moments, I long for those days with great anticipation and hope.

And then . . . I panic.

Because I know as the physical demands on my body become less and less, the emotional demands on my heart will become more and more. Toddler emotions are no match for teenage hormones. Or so I've heard.

I think it can be tempting to look at other mothers in different phases and think they have it easier than we do. *Her kids are in school six hours a day; she has so much free time! Her kids are so young and innocent; I would trade this high school drama for a preschooler in a heartbeat!*

The grass is always greener, and motherhood is no exception.

When we're in the thick of it, sometimes all we see is the hard part. We forget about the other side of the scale, even when it's tipped in our favor. Right now I'm in the stage where my back hurts more than my heart. On any given day I'm doing chores one-handed with my youngest attached to my hip. The only heartbreak we experience around here is when Mommy says no to a third episode of *Sesame Street*.

But a beautiful gift is hiding in this physically exhausting stage of parenting little children, and it's one I can often overlook when I'm tripping on Hot Wheels in the hallway at 3:00 a.m. The emotional aspect of motherhood is pretty simple in this stage. Because even on our worst days, nobody forgives like a three-year-old.

+ + +

"Everett! Let's *go*! Grab your socks!" I yell again.

I snap the baby into his car seat and pick it up with a grunt. Everett finally appears in the kitchen—barefoot—and I lose it. I start yelling about the socks, about how many times I reminded him, about how he never listens to me, about how we are always late.

He glances up at me and hesitates before barely whispering, "Mommy, my socks are right here."

He unfolds his tiny fists to reveal one blue sock tucked in each hand.

My face burns red as I kneel down to apologize. I kiss his cheek and say those two words I force him to say so often: *I'm sorry*. We sit down on the kitchen floor while I put his socks on, and he smiles at me. I open the door and he skips outside, as if nothing ever happened at all.

That's when the epiphany hits me.

My child forgives better than I do.

Oh sure, I can talk about forgiveness and grace all day long: about offering it and accepting it and extending it without stipulations. But when it comes time to put that into action, I have to admit this is where I fall short. My forgiveness usually comes slowly, stubbornly, and only after I've received a genuine, heartfelt apology.

But my three-year-old? No matter what I've done, no matter how many times I've yelled about socks or lost my patience, he forgives me. He doesn't ever say the words, but I can see it in his eyes each morning: any transgression from the previous day is gone. *Poof.* As if it never even happened. Just like my heavenly Father, my son's mercies are new for me every morning.

Later that afternoon, I am lying on the ground completely still, pretending to be asleep.

"Mommy, I'll save you!" Everett yells as he flies into my bedroom on a toy airplane. He huffs as he lodges his little body off the plastic seat.

Today I am playing the damsel in distress—I go back and forth between lying on the hardwood floor, pretending to be Sleeping Beauty, and hoisting my body behind a chair, pretending to be trapped in a dungeon.

My back is killing me.

But when this part is done—when I'm no longer playing games on the floor or carrying babies on my hip, and my body belongs to me again—when my kids grow up and my heart inevitably aches more than my back, I pray I will always remember this hidden gift.

I pray I will always remember the way my blue-eyed boy flew around the house on a toy airplane, innocent as can be, forgiving me left and right, teaching me what it means to be saved.

9

SEVEN POUNDS OF REDEMPTION

by N'tima Preusser

"Don't have a baby . . . they ruin your body," she said. I was stunned that this was the first thing she had to offer me after having raised three children. I had said I wanted to be a mother, not take up smoking. It was a shallow excuse not to bring a child into the world.

I remember being one hundred pounds. I remember hating my body. I remember being shallow too. And this was long before growing a baby was even on my radar.

I nearly killed myself for that number. I was light and frail, like a piece of old fruit shriveling up into nothing. My body hurt all the time. I wouldn't even drink water. I was always freezing.

I ONCE WAS
TOO SMALL TO
CONTAIN ALL OF
THE *love* THAT
FILLED ME.

My skin was colorless, punctuated with clogged pores, and my eyes were yellowing. My external organs were corroding as if to prove that my insides were struggling.

By the time I was seven years old, I was already coveting the face of Catherine Zeta Jones on a magazine cover. I do not know how that happens—how, as women, we go from babies blowing kisses to ourselves in the mirror to young girls pinching our bellies or dodging our reflections altogether. So many little things just added up. They went unnoticed until one day I found myself kneeling over the toilet, washing out the sound of making myself sick by running bathwater.

But my collarbones poked out, like jagged arrowheads piercing through my skin, and that is what mattered to me.

I had finally made it into the "underweight" category that I lusted after, according to the online BMI calculator that I worshipped. I was greedy for less (and less, and less). I celebrated my weakness, but I bled insecurity. The word *ugly* had a debilitating kind of dominance over me. If you had told me I was "fat," I would have come apart.

Because that is what mattered.

I was emotionally, mentally, and cellularly starving. It took me years to learn what I know now.

Between one hundred pounds and shallow, and now, deep in the trenches of motherhood, my body has borne two children—two daughters handcrafted inside my very womb. And my body still carries proof of their existences.

They each brought seven pounds of redemption, two years apart. Two tiny girls and a giant dose of clarity. It took my body swelling with child, my bones bearing the weight of another human being, the expanding, the shrinking, the scarring, the tearing—all of it—to triumph over all that my body really is.

Now I have dark pools under my eyes and a valley where my belly button once was. I stride through my days with hips my teenage self wouldn't recognize. Lines map across the mountains of stretched skin left over on my midsection; lightning bolts striking across my sides, proving I once was too small to contain all of the love that filled me. Lines indicate that my daughters once lived inside me. They are all I have left to prove that we were once one and not two.

My body, that I hated so deeply before, built my daughters' bodies.

How can I be ashamed of that?

From the moment they were placed on my chest for the first time, the responsibility to teach them how to love themselves has sat squarely, tirelessly, on my shoulders. I do not know how to vaccinate my daughters against the plague of self-hatred that runs rampant among young girls. But to my daughters, I will beg, "Fall in love with yourself, first."

And I do not mean a tolerant, conditional, praise-yourself-when-you-look-good kind of love. I mean deeply rooted, white-hot, irrevocable, laugh-at-yourself love.

This matters.

On the day my daughters look up at me, with their innocence still intact, and ask if they are pretty, I will want to shake them by the shoulders and scream, "YES!" In that pivotal moment, I will not emphasize how beautiful I think the combination of their father and I illustrated on their faces is. Instead, I will tell them that their hearts have a strength that has allowed them to live. I will not put emphasis on the nearly perfect curls in their hair or the blue that swims in their eyes. They will know, instead, that they can see, and hear, and fully taste the flavor of this life thanks to the bodies that they live in. I will emphasize the knowledge, the truth, and the creativity that they store inside their heads. I will tell them that they have bodies that are capable, bodies that are powerful. Bodies that give and give and demand nothing in return, except love.

When my daughters are on the cusp of adolescence, stricken by their first gust of insecurity, and dissecting their appearance, I hope they do not see the gap between their thighs that is or isn't there. I hope instead, that they will see looking back at them the shell of the spirit that is within. I hope they know that the number on the scale is only the numerical relationship between their bodies and gravity. That number doesn't really matter.

I will make sure that they know as women, as people, that their bodies belong to them. They will know that they do not have to be delicate or lovely if they do not want to be. I want them to know that they do not have to water themselves down to spare the intimidating of others. I hope they are unapologetic with their confidence. I hope they are a force to be reckoned with.

I want them to know that loving your body means tending to it with care. It means listening to your body, moving your body, feeding your body the things that it instinctively craves. I do not care if that means juicing organic kale or treating yourself to ice cream, as long as it is done in love.

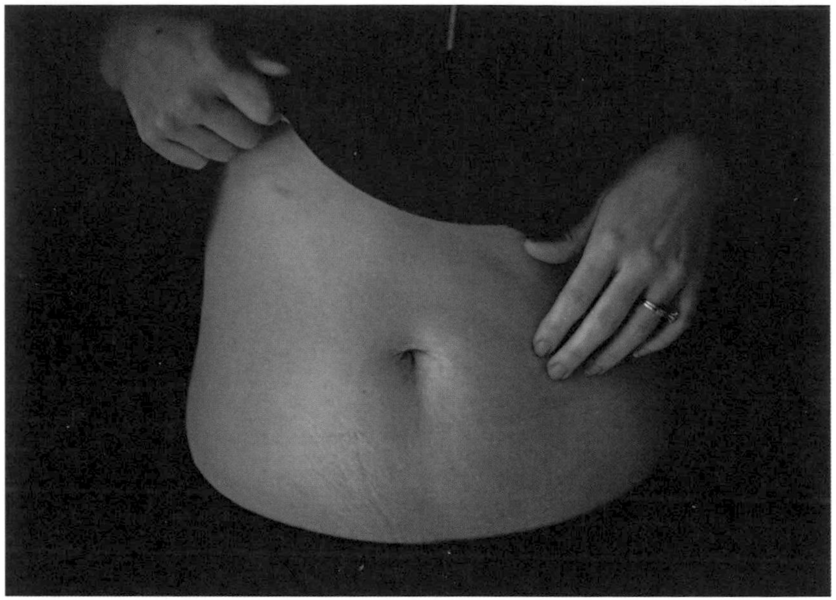

I want them to know that when they offer this kind of love, their bodies will embrace them right back. By example, I will teach them that ultimately, loving yourself is the beginning of all victories—and that is what matters.

My body is forgiving, and strong, and powerful. My body is life-giving, able, and the most accurate reflection of the goodness I carry inside of me. Having children never wrecked that truth. It couldn't. Even my daughters know my heart, they knew it before we met, and they love me for it. To them, I hang the moon. The world may have ruined me before I knew them, but they made me whole again.

THE WORLD MAY HAVE RUINED ME BEFORE I KNEW THEM, BUT THEY MADE ME *whole* AGAIN.

10

WHICH SWEATER?

by Melanie Dale

I stare into my closet, trying to find the right sweater for this meeting. Which sweater will make me feel comfy while I listen? Which sweater will make everything okay?

I let my fingers run along the edges of hangers and sleeves. The gray one buttons down the front and drapes softly to my knees. The stripey one is bright and cheery. The brown one has a cowl that makes my neck feel cozy and covers up the stress hives that break out whenever I get upset.

Better go with the cowl. Today I might get upset.

This morning I have an appointment to find out answers about my child that will change things. It will affect the trajectory of our lives. We won't be able to un-hear them or ignore them.

Maybe you've been where I am this morning. You felt shaky and nervous, but also relieved. You waited so long, weeks and weeks or maybe months, to get answers—to learn why. You're tired from not knowing. You've filled out so much paperwork that it's as if the SAT and mortgage papers mated and birthed evil paperwork spawn. Yet even with the need to know, you want to hit pause and not have to find out.

With each of my child's meltdowns and each meeting with a teacher, the truth started to dawn around the edges of my mind. Something wasn't right, but did that mean something was wrong? My child didn't "fit," but did that mean my child didn't belong? I started reading articles and checklists and talking with

other moms. All the checklists and research led to one place: this meeting.

I need the right sweater to help me cross the threshold into a new world. *Which sweater will make me feel like a grown-up? Because having a child with special needs . . . isn't that something that grown-ups handle? I'm not ready for this level of adulting.*

"Your child is on the autism spectrum."

My lungs fill with air inside my sweater. A bomb of relief explodes in my gut and floods out to my extremities. Autism. I already knew. For weeks and weeks, I felt it breaking on the horizon like an egg-yolky dawn. I feel relief that they know what we know. We're living the scene at the end of the movie when the great dramatic irony is resolved and the characters all finally know the truth.

I wanted it to be that so bad, to have an explanation for years of struggle for my child. To develop a plan. To feel the sense of satisfaction that we are not bad parents who just don't discipline well. I want to take an ad out in the paper that says, "There is a reason!"

A diagnosis comes with a plan. So I feel relief. And wrapped in the middle of the relief is something else, something I'd be lying if I said I don't feel. *Loss.*

The loss isn't really a loss—it's more of a realization that my child's life wasn't mine to live in the first place. It's a loss of expectations, which were never real, and the gain is this lovely, whole human being with a fascinating mind who teaches me to see the world through new eyes. I go to meetings and learn and ask questions. I become an advocate. Isn't that what moms are for their kids?

> **The loss isn't really a loss—it's more of a realization that my child's life wasn't mine to live in the first place.**

One day we get a letter in the mail with results from some more testing, as if there were any tests left to take. I open the letter in our smelly minivan and see more confirmation. My eyes well up with tears and I start laughing uncontrollably.

This is not my first rodeo, and I know my emotions are weird, which is why I'm sitting in the van by myself and not standing in the kitchen in front of everyone. I'm experiencing relief and joy and loss and pain at the same time, and it's not simple. I absolutely love autism, and I also want to flick it in the face. I love how it makes my child unique and interesting and funny and honest, and I hate it when my child struggles with friends and shuts down. So I laugh giddily while sobbing; it's joy-pain.

There's a lot of joy-pain going on around here. Our family has been racking up labels in the last few months. Between the five of us, we now have a collection that falls into the categories of autism, mental illness, ADHD, and trauma. If labels were tickets at an arcade, we'd have enough for the biggest stuffed animal hanging on the wall.

It's like playing Whac-a-Mole, bopping one issue down only to have another pop up in someone else. It was wearing me out. I felt . . . used up. As if after years of struggle, all my pouring out hadn't made any difference in the lives of my kids. Have you ever felt that way? You work and try and give, and at the end of the day, what do you have to show for it?

I need you to know that my kids are amazing, and I'm grateful to be their mom. And I also need you to know about the times I feel like I can't do it—because someday if you feel those scary feelings, you'll know you aren't alone. Other moms have messy feelings too, and it doesn't make us monsters. It makes us human. It makes us weak. And acknowledging that makes us strong.

I hate sports metaphors, but if ever one applied to motherhood, it's the marathon. I've only ever run a half marathon, but it was enough. I made it through mile ten before slowing to a walk. I walk-ran through the last 3.1 miles and was hospitalized later that day for an impacted colon. Sometimes motherhood feels like the first mile when you're exhilarated and flying. Sometimes it feels like a nurse shoving an enema up your patoot in the middle of the night in the geriatric ward of the county hospital.

I love motherhood. And sometimes it makes my butt hurt.

"I don't want to do this anymore. I want to quit."

My husband found me keening on the threshold of the

pantry. I was just short of reaching for the chocolate when my tears overtook me and I felt the heat pouring out of my eyes. My daughter had just poked me in the eye, really hard. It was an accident, but after spending all afternoon baking and decorating cupcakes together, playing a board game, and finally tucking her into bed and cuddling in her bunk, I was feeling really proud of this mom thing. I worked so hard. And here at the finish line for the day, she poked, I yelped in pain, and she turned her little body away from me, face pressed into her pillow. After four hours of togetherness, we were further apart than when we started.

You know when you're crying about your eye getting poked but you're really crying about so much more? After months of hard conversations with the team of doctors and therapists surrounding our family, my very bones felt exhausted. I wanted to quit. If motherhood is a ministry, I wanted a new ministry. Maybe I'd be better at being a greeter at church or singing in a choir or something. This was just too hard.

What's a battle-weary mother to do?

I wish I had a 12-step plan, but here's one thing that's helping me: I'm becoming a collector of moments. As we swerve in and out of appointments and tweak strategies and develop systems, I spend each day searching for moments worth savoring.

We had a family dance party in the kitchen after dinner, and one of my kids did the robot and one did the dab and one stood on a bench and twirled. One afternoon, my child who struggles with fear and receiving love agreed to be held. And I held and swaddled and caressed her face and poured in all the love I could during that small window. Around the dinner table I read a few pages of a biography, and when I stopped, my kids said, "Just a few more pages, Mommy." Yesterday I pulled my oldest, with feet almost as big as mine, onto my lap and kissed her head.

I think savoring *every* moment is too much pressure. But I'm scooping up the moments worth savoring, and I'm peeling back the diagnoses in our family to reveal the beautiful individuals underneath.

We can laugh. We can dance. We can hug. I remember.

It's not easy mothering with labels, but I am so thankful that those labels don't define our kids. With every new label and diagnosis, nothing changed and everything changed. My kids were the exact same kids they were before I put on those sweaters and walked into those rooms. And now we have knowledge and a plan. While we do have to go through it, we don't have to let it wreck us.

These labels we receive for our kids are the beginning and not the end. They are opportunities to find help or healing, and while our families will adapt and change, we won't despair.

Yes, sometimes I do want to quit, but I never will. I've been learning to take care of myself while I'm taking care of my kids. And then I snuggle into a sweater and show up every day, and show up, and show up some more.

If you have been where I am, receiving a diagnosis for one of your precious babies, you should know: you are loved. Friend, we are fierce. Our hearts beat strongly inside our sweaters. We can do this together because God has given us each other.

11

THE GLITTER AND THE GLUE

by Anna Quinlan

"Your father was the glitter but I was the glue." That's the explanation behind the title of *Glitter and Glue*, the "heartfelt homage to motherhood" written by Kelly Corrigan. The first time I heard it, I felt like she must have been spying on my life, that she must have observed the exact parenting dynamic in our home.

When it comes to motherhood, I don't have a lot of glitter. I don't do summer bucket lists or busy bags or special "dates" with my kids. They are three and four and a half right now, and these preschool years are hard for me. My boys are willful and wild and illogical, as is to be expected, I guess. They've

also recently discovered the joy of shouting the word *fart* at each other, and . . . I just can't. I shake my head and walk out of the room.

My husband, though, he is all glitter. He is fun and patient and able to act interested in fart jokes. He's a wizard at Legos and never adds peas to boxed mac and cheese. He will "watch this!" infinitely and act just as impressed on the twenty-seventh jump as he did on the first. They adore him. We all do. Sometimes I'm jealous of what a natural he is, of how easily he seems to weather their tornado of toddlerdom. On my bad days, I resent him a little bit. I wish I got to be the fun one, but I'm not right now. I'm the glue.

I know the schedule and the contact information and where

the other shoe is. I remember to wash the blanket that comes home from preschool on Friday and bring it back on Monday. I know that we have to buy more laundry soap this week if anyone wants clean underwear, and that we should eat the rest of that watermelon before it starts to ferment in about two days. They would basically be boxcar children without me. They'd be happy, but they'd be feral. I am the glue, and we all know it.

Sometimes I worry that my lack of glitter means that I matter less to them. I don't expect them to appreciate all that the glue does right now—they are preschoolers, for crying out loud—but I worry that they might not see the ways I show my love. I worry that I'm fading into the background sometimes, no flashy Lego buildings or fart jokes to attract their spotlight.

I worry that they might not see the ways I show my love. I worry that I'm fading into the background sometimes.

A few weeks ago, my four-year-old developed a bad case of chapped lips. I tried to apply ointment several times throughout the day, but it was mostly futile because, well, he's four. I figured I could sneak into his bedroom and smear one last application of Aquaphor on him in his sleep, though, since those nighttime hours are the only time he's not talking and moving with breakneck enthusiasm.

So on my way to bed, exhausted, I tiptoe into his room. I

climb the ladder into his top bunk and carefully move his legs to untangle the blanket and pull it up around him. He feels floppy in my arms, not like the active little boy that he was just a few hours ago, but like the baby that I used to rock to sleep. I put a dab of ointment on my finger and touch it to his lips.

He stirs. Without opening his eyes he turns his head and croaks, "Mom?"

I am surprised to feel a lump in my throat at the sound of his gravelly whisper. Something about it is exactly the reassurance that I didn't even know I needed. He knows it's me. He didn't open his eyes, but he knows that it's me who's crawled into his top bunk in the middle of the night, worrying about him and knowing the remedy. Even in his sleep he knows that it's my body next to him, my hands cupping his face, my tiptoes across the floor. It's not flashy or fun or glittery, but it's still my true love for him.

And he feels it.

12

THE MOM THEY NEED

by Katie Blackburn

Not long ago I found myself in a blissful state of motherhood. I was enjoying trips to Target with one seven-month-old in tow, watching her play contentedly, cooing and giggling along with her as she started to find her own voice. I was putting her to bed and not hearing from her again for ten to twelve hours most nights, and making her real baby food for breakfast when she woke up. We had our routines, the special ways that only the two of us could communicate, and for a moment, I sure thought we had it down, the whole mother-daughter thing. We would be best friends forever, no doubt about it.

But everyone warned me it would change.

YOU
ARE
MY
WILD

Other moms loved to tell me stories like, "Ryan has been biting at preschool," or "Anna threw her whole body down in line at the grocery store when I said no to the Tic Tacs," or my favorite, "If you think two-year-olds are hard, just wait for three. Someone should have named it the terrible threes."

Hmmm. It must be tough, I thought in response to these stories, with no actual empathy in my mind. Because in my case, parenting my not-yet-walking daughter was, dare I say, easy. She didn't speak, she didn't move much, and she slept all night long. I actually remember thinking, *Come on, people! How hard can this be?*

Never, ever ask that question.

Because everything did change. One day at a time, *easy* stopped being a thing around here.

I noticed the strong sense of independence in my daughter right around her first birthday. While many other little girls her age seemed compliant, shy, and calm, mine was not any of those things. She knew what she wanted, and by sixteen months old she was saying, "By self!" as a disclaimer to every demand.

And then there was "the playdate"—a day that will live in infamy. We were at a dear friend's home, whose daughter is only three weeks older than mine. We settled in with a cup of coffee and sent the kids, the two girls and one older brother, to the other room to play. Less than ten minutes into our conversation, I heard crying, followed quickly by a report from the older brother in the room: "Mom, Harper hit Evelyn!"

"Oh gosh, I'm so sorry! Let me go talk to her!" I unfolded

my legs, set my coffee on the end table, and quickly ran into the other room to investigate.

"Harper, did you hit Evelyn? Harper, we don't hit people. Please give her back that toy."

I returned to my cozy corner on the couch, reoriented myself to our conversation, and again, within minutes, there was more yelling, more reporting, more reproofing of my daughter. After the fourth time I got up, we decided to move into the room with the kids.

But that only forced me to see what the five-year-old big brother had been reporting all along: *my daughter was acting terrible*. She was stealing toys, hitting her friend, and had no regard for the correction her momma was trying to give her. It was the first time I felt actual embarrassment as a mother, the first time I felt ashamed, and the first time I desperately wanted someone to show me the empathy that I hadn't given to others. We left our friend's home after less than an hour, my daughter convulsing in anger because I ripped the fairy wings out of her hand as we left, and my head hanging in shame at what had just happened.

Do I have a bad child? Does my friend think I have a bad child? Am I a bad mom? Does my friend think I am a bad mom? Is everything just always going to be BAD?

A similar pattern of punishment hung around our home for months: my daughter behaved badly, I got angry. She responded with more bad behavior; I responded with more anger. It was day after day of tantrum, time-out, lecture, tantrum, time-out, lecture, and a weary set of parents wondering what we had actually signed up for. Something I could not name was just not working. I sought advice from friends, got pep talks from mentors, read all the books, and regularly started praying for help. Because the truth was—*I never thought it would be so hard to be a mom.*

A sweet mentor texted me one morning and gave me the beautiful gift of asking how she could pray for me. Through tears I responded, telling her how timely her request was, how being a mom was nothing like I thought it would be when I registered for those soft pink crib sheets. And then I asked her to pray for wisdom for me, because I wanted to do something different. I wanted to do something that would break up the pattern of tantrum to time-out that we were living in. But I had no idea what that something was.

I liked the real version of motherhood better than the fairy tale anyway, because the real version was forcing me to be smaller so God could get bigger.

Then she said this: "Katie, God gave me a feisty daughter too. And I remember the hardest part of her little years was that, sometimes, I had to become a mom I didn't want to be. Hang in there, though, because you are the mom she needs."

A mom I didn't want to be. But the mom she needs.

Those became life-changing words for me.

Slowly, change started to happen in our home, but it was mostly a change in me. I began to see motherhood as a much bigger narrative than the idyllic stories I'd told myself.

Being the mom my baby girl needed sometimes meant forty-five minutes of me repeatedly walking from the top of the stairs to the time-out spot at the bottom, putting my hand on the back of an angry and inconsolable little girl, reminding her that I am still there and that I still love her like crazy. Sometimes it meant leaving playdates, while other times it meant canceling them altogether. And still other times, it meant asking for forgiveness from a three-year-old, because I was the one who had thrown a fit.

None of these things was on my mind as I felt her precious baby kicks in my belly. One hardly imagines the emotional holes motherhood can pull us into while we are decorating the nursery. But as I started to let go of the fairy tale I thought motherhood would be, I stepped into the story God was really writing, and grew into the mom my daughter needed.

I liked the real version of motherhood better than the fairy tale anyway, because the real version was forcing me to be smaller so God could get bigger. And isn't that what He intended all along?

We've added two more babies to our family since my mentor gave me that good advice, but her words have only become truer. Each precious child has challenged me to let go of the vision of the mom I wanted to be so I could be the mom my kids need.

The longer we parent, the better we get at this role change. It's not just about learning to discipline well; it's about learning that love is made real when it is tested, in the times we have to be someone we never thought we would be. When our daughter experiences something hard, when our son has trouble learning, when the doctor comes into the room with a diagnosis, when our children make decisions we taught them for years not to make . . . in those moments when the story is not reading how we always wanted it to, that's when we have to remember that we are *still* the right person for the role. Because with every step of this motherhood journey, through prayer and patience and learning to trust our own intuition, we *can be* the mommas our kids need.

13

BAD MATH

by April Hoss

It's the same two questions on every form: number of pregnancies, number of children. My answers shine back at me impassively, not unlike fresh blood: 2, 0. Two pregnancies. Zero children.

That's some bad math.

My first pink line popped into view on July 15, 2011. I know this because I took the test on a whim just before heading out the door to meet friends for the last Harry Potter film. A sign if ever there was one! Our dogs are named Sirius Black and Lily. Major fandom happening here. And it had been so easy, like magic. We tried on a whim, and after one month, *boom*. Pregnant. One plus one would equal a family of three. Good math.

By August 21 things looked much different. I was at a birthday party, and I remember studying the sun as it set in a purple sky while the cake was served. I excused myself before taking a bite, hoping I'd imagined the sudden sense of cold. I'm not sure who threw away my slice when I left the party in a panic. Several days of horrific uncertainty and equally horrific tests would pass before I was declared un-pregnant. Then, on a Saturday morning, five days after the abandoned birthday cake, I would drive from a gas station to the ER, soaked in my own blood, my car seat filling with it. More doctors, more tests, and into the operating room I went. I had to sign a waiver acknowledging I understood I may never conceive again. The nurses offered me warm socks after that.

They were no use. I stayed cold from the birthday party till Christmas.

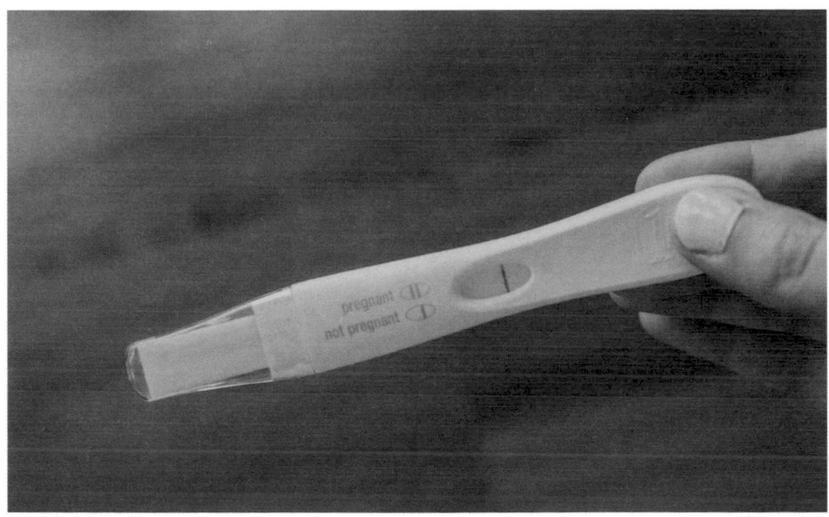

Flash forward to July 15, 2012. In the most unbelievable, downright bizarre twist of circumstances, I got another pink line. Two months of trying plus one vacation and—*boom*. Pregnant. A pink plus sign said it was so. Maybe now I could balance the equation of the year before.

This one was going to make it, of course. Any other alternative was too cruel to be possible. No, this pregnancy would go the distance, and come March 2013, I'd be back in that same hospital, only this time I'd be holding my baby, not signing liability forms.

But the story is in the numbers, right? My husband and I went together for my first doctor appointment sometime mid-August. Given my *unfortunate history* I was given an ultrasound on the spot. We stared in wonder at our tiny, blinking miracle. I remembered the waiver and smiled. The OB seemed far less victorious. She said our baby had a slow heartbeat, then moved her face closer to the black and green screen. She ordered tests. My numbers should be doubling, she said. I would get blood drawn that day, and then again two days later.

I flunked this math test too, like so many before it. My numbers didn't double; they hardly increased at all. A second ultrasound showed no heartbeat. By now it was late August, the twenty-first, exactly one year later from my first miscarriage. Impossible.

What are the chances? Seriously, I would like to know the exact probability of that happening to a person. Talk about bad math.

So with a deep sense of irony and an even deeper sense of

despair, I began my second miscarriage. I say *began* because the thing about having a miscarriage is that it's not over when it's over. First comes the medical miscarriage. Then, after all the exams and appointments and text messages, after all the nurses and doctors and medical residents inspecting you and talking about next steps (as well as casually, innocently asking who wants burritos for lunch, because this is their job and they see it every day and who can blame them), comes the emotional miscarriage. Your schedule clears up, no more running around town trying to save this little human you already love so much. But your inbox fills. So many "I'm sorrys" to read. So many "Thank yous" to send. You reply with so many "I appreciate its" and "We're good with meals." They mean it. They are sorry. And you are sorry. Sorrow all around. Sorrow everywhere. You wonder if that is what you are—a billion cells of sorrow.

By the latest calculations I'd had two miscarriages in twelve months. Things got weird. Lots of Netflix. Lots of homemade margaritas. An endless parade of yoga pants and worn college sweatshirts. My husband watched me from the kitchen; then he watched with me, from the couch.

I noticed though, around the first edges of spring, that I was starting to feel different. Not better—forget better; better is beside the point. Different, that's reasonable. Because you may never feel better. I don't. That's the other thing about having a miscarriage: a miscarriage may very well start to have you. It robs you physically and emotionally, ransacking your gut and your heart. Then it sets its sights on your head. It will rummage through all of your drawers. Having taken much of your dignity, some of your dreams, and more tears than you can count, it looks for what else it can steal.

My husband and I brought our son home two Novembers after miscarriage number one. We'd been journeying toward him since we were teenagers, talking about adoption over nachos and Cherry Cokes. Do you know that miscarriage compels me to overexplain how much he is loved and wanted? I feel the need to let everyone know we started the adoption process two years before I ever became pregnant, and that our beautiful boy is by no means some consolation prize or plan B, but our teenage dream come true. See? There I go again. I am not better. Different. Not better.

There's something else too. Something I am afraid to talk about because people will think I'm crazy, or worse, cliché. On that birthday party night, the first time subtraction got the best of me, something happened around midnight. By that point I'd been bleeding for a while and we'd sent all the texts to all our people. The hospital told me to come back the next morning; nothing could be done. So I lay wide awake in the dark, weeping intermittently and getting really angry. And then I heard God speak to me.

I know, I know.

I am not saying if my mom or my friends or my coworkers were in the room, they would have heard a voice from above. They wouldn't have. I didn't hear an audible sound; nothing shook or began to smoke. No smells, no bells. I am saying that in my dark night of the soul, my heart heard two words: *Keep reading*.

Keep reading. I clung to those words. Through the rest of the night and the rest of the tests and the rest of the year and all the way through the next terrible August, my knuckles turned white around those words, *keep reading.* I held tight to the God who had to tell me over and over I was not a bad math problem. I was, I am, a story. One I'm still trying to read. And like all stories, there are good parts and sad parts, chapters that make me shift in my seat and scowl, plotlines I wish I could edit. But the ending is guaranteed to be good, and I can trust the Author.

I held tight to the God who had to tell me over and over I was not a bad math problem. I was, I am, a story.

This is what made me feel different (not better). This is what got me off the couch, off Netflix, and back to me. A stronger, more scarred, more excited version of me. I kept the warm socks on, and I turned the page.

I'd love to pass out warm socks with the little sticky things on the sole to every woman in the midst of a bad math problem of her own. I would say, "Hear this: You are not bad math. You are not the nine weeks you can't get past or the three years you've been trying or the twins you never got to meet or the one-child family you never wanted to be. You might *have* terrible math, but you *are not* terrible math. You are a story. You are a work in progress. You are on the way to feeling different; in two months or two years or two decades, you will wake up to yourself again. Keep reading.

14

PROFILE OF A SUPERHERO

by Callie R. Feyen

My seven-year-old, Harper, and I are on a walk. She's picking up rocks and putting them in her pocket, a practice she's started so she can remember where she's been: Chicago, Raleigh, Grand Rapids, Germantown. She keeps them in a Mason jar in her bedroom. At first, she'd write the date and the place on the rock. Lately though, she holds it in the palm of her hand for a moment, then names it: Aqua Marine, Double Vampire, Baby Lava.

Today she has a quartz-looking rock between her thumb and finger. She's holding it up to the sky and watching it twinkle.

"What will you name this one?" I ask Harper.

"Broken Beauty," she says without a moment's hesitation. "See?" She puts the stone in my palm gently. "It's broken, I think," she explains as she points to a part that looks like it's been chipped off, like it belonged to something bigger. "But it is still so beautiful," she says with her hands on her knees and her face close to my hand. I can feel her breath on my palm.

"I think that's a perfect name," I tell Harper. She plucks Broken Beauty from my hand and puts it in her pocket.

"You know what I'm really good at?" she asks me, holding my hand as we walk.

"What?"

"I'm really good at taking a small thing and turning it into a really big deal."

"You are really good at that," I say, laughing. "It's like a superpower."

We walk in silence for a while. I watch Harper study the sidewalk, the sky, the trees. "Mommy," Harper whispers, "it *is* like a superpower!"

A few hours later it is bedtime, and I'm helping my girls get ready. I wish this were a peaceful part of the day, but it is not. Everyone is tired, and nobody wants to cooperate, including me. Hadley and Harper have PhDs in stalling, which makes my already-thin patience practically nonexistent. Things that don't bother me in the morning drive me crazy at night.

"Did you feed your fish?" I ask while Hadley and Harper are changing.

"Yup," Hadley says.

"I didn't," Harper says, and I immediately scold her.

"Harper! You have to feed your fish! It'll die if you don't feed it."

"I'll just get another one," she says, skipping to the bathroom to brush her teeth.

"No! You won't! You've named him," I say, pointing to the tank where Flick the fish lives. "You leave him notes and bring in rocks for him to look at. You don't want him to die. That's not how you treat a living thing!" She looks at me, her smile gone, and walks slowly to get the fish food.

She carefully takes four pellets and plunks them in one at a time, waiting for Flick to gobble each one up before she drops

another in. Her eyes are wide to stop her tears from dropping, and also from the shock at what I've said about death. Her mouth is quivering. I have blown Flick's nutritional needs way out of proportion.

"Harper," I say pulling her to my lap. "I'm sorry. You are a great friend to Flick, and I know you just forgot to feed him today. I am sorry I got angry and said those things."

"It's okay, Mommy," she says, but the tears are falling now. They fall on our fingers, intertwined and holding on to each other.

"You know your special thing?" I say. "The one where you take something small and make it into something big?"

Harper looks at me and nods.

"I have that too. Sometimes, I don't use it for good. Tonight was one of those times, and I am sorry."

The great thing about seven-year-olds is that forgiveness is swift and pairs with forgetfulness. Harper is skipping and twirling about ninety seconds later. I, on the other hand, sit on the couch for the rest of the evening and ruminate.

The great thing about seven-year-olds is that forgiveness is swift and pairs with forgetfulness.

I envy Harper because she thinks her ability to make small things big is a gift. I don't think I've ever recognized it as such. I think it's something that hurts and annoys others. At best I get called dramatic and imaginative with friendly nudges and shakes of the head.

I didn't mean to pass this on to Harper, but I believe there is truth in what I told her about having a superpower. What we have is powerful: we can make people see things they didn't know were there. We have the ability to bring amazement and wonder to the broken pieces of beauty we hold up to the sky.

I also know the sadness and anger this trait can bring. I don't want to pass on a superpower that becomes a burden.

The next day, I am in the woods with a bunch of middle school students. We're on a field trip, participating in one of those all-day risk-taking, face-your-fears excursions. I hate these things. They're always in nature. Why can't I face my fears taking the metro or ordering a coffee during rush hour in the city? But here I am, facing a tree with about ten huge staples in it, and a three-by-four-foot platform nailed to its trunk about thirty-five feet above the ground. Our leader, Craig, is wrapping a cord around his waist and telling us that we are going to climb the tree, get on the platform, and jump off. We will hold on to the cord, and somehow the balance of his weight will make us glide gracefully to the ground.

"Okay, guys!" I say, clapping. "You got this!" I shove my seventh graders toward Craig. One by one, each of them climbs up the tree and jumps, until Craig says to me, "You're next."

"Yeah, Mrs. Feyen! You're next!" Seventh graders are slapping me on the back. One of them takes his helmet off and puts it on my head. It is sweaty, and I think I'm going to throw up. Craig checks the knots and clips on my harness as I shake and breathe as though I'm in labor. I hope I don't have to say it, that he will understand how terrified I am and pretend the rope broke, or there's a bear in the woods, and call the whole thing off. This does not happen.

The first task is to climb up a ladder to get to the first staple. I say that's all I'm going to do—get off the ladder—then I'm coming down.

"Okay," Craig says.

But I'm halfway up the tree once I get off the ladder, so I keep going.

The tree and the staples are slippery from the rain, and I am far from the ground. I'm so high, my students look like Charlie Brown characters. With one more push I can get to the platform, but it involves a bit of a leg swing and arm rearranging. I don't want to move. I can't stop shaking. I can feel my throat swell and my eyes brim with tears. I am terrified. "I think I need to come down," I yell to Craig. "I don't think I can do this."

My students cheer me on. "You're so close! You can do it, Mrs. Feyen!"

Craig says nothing.

"I need to come down," I say, and I hate myself for letting my students see me like this: terrified and crying and quitting.

"You can come down," Craig says. "But what you're feeling is fear."

No duh, I think.

"You're afraid," he says again. "But you're safe. If you come down, you will be making a decision based on fear. Are you gonna let your fear decide what you do next?"

He doesn't finish that question before I start to climb. My body answers for me. It's like everything in it was screaming, "*No!*"

My students are screaming for me as I step onto the platform and stand up. The air is thin and sweet, and the leaves are lime green for the start of spring.

I take a deep breath and jump.

I sail to the bottom feeling like a superhero.

I tell Hadley and Harper what I did today when I pick them up from school. I am jubilant. "I was so scared, but I did it anyway!" I look at their reaction in the rearview mirror: Hadley has a big grin on her face, and Harper's eyes are wide.

As we drive, I wonder if I made this a bigger deal than it really is. After all, a bunch of twelve-and thirteen-year-olds did the same thing I did.

Maybe the tree wasn't that high.

Maybe the air wasn't that sweet.

Maybe I shouldn't have been that afraid.

Maybe it wasn't that big of a deal.

Once home, I unlock the door and we walk inside. The girls throw their backpacks on the floor, grab boxes of chocolate milk, and run outside to play. Hadley rides her bike down a hill with a neighbor boy. Harper and two girls climb a weeping willow. I watch them and think back to a couple of hours ago when I was standing on that platform and looking around. The air really was sweet, and my fear was real. Remnants of it still prickle the hairs on my arms. I kind of like it.

At bedtime, I'm helping the girls get ready again when Harper tells me that she'd like to go skydiving someday.

"Won't you be scared?" I ask, pulling off her T-shirt and handing her a nightgown.

"Yeah, I'll be scared," Harper says, but her voice is confident and steady. "But I can do it because I have what you have."

"What's that?" I ask, kneeling down and searching her blue eyes. *What good thing did I pass on to you, sweet girl?*

"You were scared, but you did it anyway. I have that too."

"Yes, you do," I tell her.

One day, Harper might forget about her superpowers, but I'll remind her. I'll show her again and again how to use them. Because that's what mothers, and superheroes, do.

15

TRUST AND FORGOTTEN LUNCHES

by Lesley Miller

There is no hour of the day more stressful than seven to eight in the morning when I balance eight hundred various tasks, including but not limited to: flipping pancakes, finding the missing shoe, changing the poopy diaper—twice sometimes—fixing the library book binding, dispersing Pteranodon vitamins ("*Not* the T. rex, Mom!"), calming an irrationally hysterical two-year-old, making lunches, and maybe, if I'm lucky, putting on eyebrow gel . . . a crucial and necessary step in making me feel like a woman rather than a personal chef and housecleaner.

A few weeks ago my mother-in-law came to help for the day, which meant that our usual morning chaos was slightly better and worse all at the same time. She helped get breakfast ready, and I made lunches while we chatted. Before I knew it though, we were running late. (When will I learn there is never time for chitchat when trying to get out the door before 8:00 a.m.?) This was definitely a morning without eyebrow gel.

It wasn't until we pulled into the preschool parking lot that I realized we'd forgotten my four-year-old daughter's backpack and lunch. In her short school career, we'd never forgotten a lunch, and while I knew there'd be plenty more instances like this one, it felt like a defeat. I even had extra help getting out the door! With no time to return home, I promised her a special treat instead.

"How about I pick up a PB&J box at Starbucks for you today?" I said, as if this had been my plan all along. I work part-time as a freelance writer, and the Starbucks closest to preschool often acts as my office.

My sweet child took the bait.

"A lunch from *Starbucks*? Oh yes, Mommy! Yes!" she said, skipping down the steps to her classroom, thrilled by the rare treat of a take-out meal.

I promised her that I'd drop off food before her class started eating, and she asked no further questions. On my way to the car, I popped my head into the preschool director's office to confirm what time lunch started. My plan was perfect.

With my eyes on the clock all morning, I sat at Starbucks and barreled through deadlines and assignments, constantly aware that I couldn't run late. At 11:35 I scooped up a PB&J box with carrots and apple slices—ironically the same lunch sitting on our counter at home—and headed back to school for the noon deadline. I didn't want her to worry that I'd forgotten about her, so I planned to show up five minutes before lunch started. But when I walked into the classroom, everyone was already eating. Twelve little bodies, wiggly and loud, compared their lunches while discussing important things like juice boxes and *Dinosaur Train*. My sweet girl sat at her seat, hands folded on the table, observing the action. My heart sank thinking how concerned she must have been, waiting and wondering if her food would ever come.

I rushed in the door with a flustered smile. She gave me a huge grin of her own.

"I'm so sorry I'm late, sweet girl," I said, handing her the lunch box. She grabbed it eagerly.

"It's okay!" she said back, without concern.

Her teacher smiled at me.

"I offered her some of my lunch, but she assured me that you'd be here soon. She wasn't worried."

I pictured Anna, just moments before, turning down the teacher's kind offer. *My mommy will be here. My mommy is coming. My mommy can be trusted.* Tears filled my eyes as I realized her complete confidence in my capabilities as a mom.

I think back to the early days of motherhood, when her needs were constant and unclear—that first night in the hospital when I'd fed her, changed her, swaddled her, and she was still crying. That first weekday morning alone with her at home. That evening when our friends came over for dinner and I bounced her in the living room, at a loss for how to soothe her anxious wails. She was upset and I was too. Would I ever be the mom she needed, or was I not cut out for this parenting gig?

I think back to the first night we let her cry it out. I stared at the ceiling, heart pounding and hands sweating, nervous she'd never trust me again. I think back to the first time we left her with grandparents for the weekend, and she ignored me when we returned forty-eight hours later, burying her head in Grandma's shoulder instead of running to me like I thought she would. I think back to all the times over the last four years that we've made decisions we know are best for her long-term growth, but at the time made her feel weary and unsure—the traumatic swim lessons she eventually came to love, the long-fought battle to accept the church nursery, and the idea that using a potty is indeed a cleaner experience than diapers.

There's a bookshelf full of motherhood insecurities in the stores of my brain, and she, in that moment at her preschool lunch table, shrugs them off. *No big deal that you're late. I trust you, Momma.*

In that moment I realize that her trust muscles, while tinier than mine, might actually be much stronger. It's as if she's thrown out every hard moment and instead only stores the ways I've met her needs and showed her the way. All the late-night feeds. The approximately five thousand meals I've made since her first year of life. The ways I rush to her when she falls on the playground. The times I rubbed oils all over her feverish body. How I'm rarely late to pick her up. I fail at times, of course, but in the grand picture of her life, I give her few reasons to doubt that I'm a person she can trust.

I hug her tightly before leaving the classroom, awed at the little lesson she's taught me without knowing. I have my own Father, a great Provider of love and comfort, but oftentimes I remember the pain more than I remember the provision. I remember the horrible moments of waiting more than the glorious ways He answers.

Moment after moment in my own life, God continues to show up when I need Him—providing for us financially, healing our bodies, healing our hearts. But sometimes in my small worldview, He runs far too late. Sometimes, I question whether He will even show up at all. With every health crisis, and every friend who gets a bad diagnosis, and every terrible car accident and every terrorist attack and every baby lost—my trust in God is tested. We all do it, I think. We lose trust that He will show up at the right time, with the right lunch, just as promised. But that's silly, really, because my belief in God is not one of blind faith. I can see His consistent, loving character in the words of my Bible and the pages of my aging journals, which hold story after story of answered prayers and modern-day miracles.

I want to be more like my preschooler, who waited with eager and confident expectation for what she knew was promised.

And in the moments when I do let her down—because I will continue to, despite my best efforts—I'm thankful to know that while I might not always be mom enough, God will always be big enough. He can always be trusted. He's always on time. He will always show up, for her and for me.

16

A SKY FULL OF GRACE

by Ashlee Gadd

The sound of a tire rolling on gravel still haunts me. I see flashes: the sunset, the river, my double stroller with two kids strapped in it barreling toward the water. My body hitting the ground. The scar. The blood swirling down the shower drain.

I get knots in my stomach just thinking about that day.

It was a typical Thursday. After weighing witching hour strategies—an early bath, early dinner, or a walk outside—the sunshine streaming through the windows made the decision easy.

"Everett, go get your gigi!" I instructed my oldest. A minute later, he ran into the kitchen with his threadbare blue blanket trailing on the ground behind him. I grabbed an applesauce pouch from the snack cabinet before strapping Everett into the left side of our new double stroller, clicking Carson in his car seat into the right side. It was warm out, but I pulled a teal knotted hat over Carson's head and tucked a light blanket over his eight-pound body for good measure. I stared at the double BOB stroller, slightly astounded that such an impressive piece of baby gear belonged to *me*. I was still getting used to the size and weight of it all—both the stroller and the fact that I was a mother of two.

We strolled down the driveway and veered left at the end of our street toward the elevated river trail. If we hurried, we would probably be able to catch the sunset. I pushed the heavy stroller up the steep, tree-lined path, feeling the weight of two kids in every muscle in my legs.

With one last push, we arrived at the top, and the view was stunning as usual.

"Look, Everett! Do you see that pretty sunset?"

I motioned toward the sun, which was probably fifteen minutes away from disappearing altogether. I made a mental note to take a picture of the sky on the way back.

We walked along the trail and said hi to every passerby: joggers, cyclists, a few college students strolling toward campus, a man walking his dog. Carson fell asleep while Everett chattered, joyfully pointing out every single thing he witnessed: "Look, Momma! A bird! A butterfwy! An airpwane!"

About half a mile in, we turned around, and I almost gasped at the view. The whole sky had morphed into an abstract painting.

Orange and pink hues swirled the heavens, with billowy cloud strokes added for texture. Beautiful sunsets are no stranger to the river trail, but that day, the sky was exceptional. I reveled in it: that moment, those two sweet boys in the stroller, the warm breeze on my face. *Not too shabby for a witching hour.*

Just before we arrived at the path that led back down to our neighborhood, I stopped the stroller to take a picture. I pulled my phone from the cup holder and turned around to face the sunset. The trail fell silent. All of the college students and joggers had vanished, leaving me with a perfect, magnificent view of the sky.

Click.

It happened in a second, two seconds tops.

I only heard the sound of a tire rolling on gravel.

My head whipped around as I watched my double stroller tip over the ledge of the path and start falling in slow motion, heading straight toward the river.

I was not even able to scream.

My body launched down the hill at full speed trailing just one foot behind them with my arm outstretched, aching, praying, pleading, *Please, God. Please, God. Please, God.*

I tripped on a rock and fell flat to the ground, but my body sprang up as if it never happened. The stroller slowed a bit and crashed into a shrub. I yanked the handlebar back, gasping for air, desperate for a sight of them.

Everett looked stunned. Carson slept through the whole thing.

"Everett . . . are you okay?!" I managed to get out, still gasping.

He nodded. I looked over at Carson in the car seat, his body lightly covered with leaves and mini pine needles. I touched his face, his hands, and watched him inhale and exhale a few times.

Hot tears streamed down my face as the adrenaline began to wear off. I started to feel my body again, my fingers and toes. I was covered in dirt from the fall, and there was a huge bleeding gash on the left side of my hip. My hands were studded with little rocks and my legs were covered in cuts. Everything hurt. I looked around for help, but there was not a single person in sight.

I spotted my phone at the bottom of the hill and called my husband to tell him what happened. I reassured him that we were all fine, but I was lying through my teeth.

I was anything but fine.

I checked the kids again and made sure they were okay before placing my trembling hands back on the handlebars. I started pushing the stroller back up the hill, startled by the pain in my knees.

Demons pounced on the silence.

How could you have been that stupid, that reckless? Why didn't you put the brake on the stroller? Why did you take your hands off the handlebar? Why did you turn away from them? Why did you need that dumb picture? What if the stroller had gone past the shrub? What if the stroller had fallen in the river? What if? What if?

I blinked back tears and tried to rationalize with myself, desperate to obliterate that hypothetical. My own voice broke the silence.

"Everett, Mommy is so sorry. Was that really scary?"

"Yeah . . . that was scawy," his little voice squeaked. "But I just held my gigi weally tight."

I stopped the stroller and burst into fresh tears at the image of my two-and-a-half-year-old holding on to his blue blanket for dear life in a moment of overwhelming fear.

I walked to the front of the stroller and knelt down beside him, my knees aching from the fall.

"Ev, Mommy is so, so sorry. That was *very* scary. Mommy was scared too. It was just an accident," I reassured him, while desperately trying to reassure myself.

The three of us made the short trek back to our house, and I prayed the whole way home. Three lines, over and over again. *Thank You, God, for protecting my babies. Please forgive me. Please help me to forgive myself.*

As soon as we got home, I turned on an episode of *Sesame Street* in a futile attempt at normalcy. In the bathroom, I carefully removed my clothes to find even more cuts and bruises.

I stepped into the shower and let warm water fall over me, but nothing could wash away the horror of what had just happened. I couldn't separate the scalding water hitting my face from my own hot tears. I put my hands on the wall of the shower for support while my body shook with sobs.

Three days later, I went back to the river trail with my husband. I pointed out where I fell, and where the stroller had crashed. We examined the scene together, and for the very first time, I realized how much space was between the river and where we were standing.

"Babe, that stroller *never* would have made it to the river. Even if you had stopped chasing it, the stroller would have stopped by itself."

He was right. The worst scenarios I had fabricated in my head would have been physically impossible. I forced the vision of my double stroller sinking to the bottom of the river out of my head once and for all.

I wish I could say that eliminating the worst-case hypothetical made it easier to forgive myself, but it didn't.

The wound on my hip eventually healed, but one year later, I have a permanent scar there, about the size of a quarter—a relentless purple mark to remind me of that day. Sometimes I think about getting it laser removed, like a regrettable tattoo. At first glimpse, it's a painful reminder of my own carelessness—tangible proof of my worst day as a mother.

It's taken a whole year (and a whole lot of prayer) to see something different, but now when I look at my body in the mirror, at second glimpse, I am learning to see this truth: *every scar on my body tells a story*. Each line, stretch mark, scar, and blemish on my skin carries the evidence of my love for these children: a love that stretches, a love that is willing to be sliced open on a metal table, a love that would run full speed down a hill without breathing. This love doesn't stand by to watch. It is not helpless. This love is a wholehearted participant.

And yet, these scars on my body also serve as a not-so-beautiful reminder of my own humanity, evidence that I am made of flesh—flawed, imperfect, and breakable. When I put that into perspective, it makes my Creator's love for me that much greater. Unlike us, our heavenly Father is not prone to accidents or even capable of making mistakes. His love for His children is full, whole, and divinely perfect. I never understood how loved I was by God until I became a mother and realized this truth: the love I have for my children pales in comparison to the love God has for me. Just thinking about that takes my breath away.

It's a new day, and a new witching hour. We're up at the river trail again. The boys are both inhaling applesauce pouches, and Carson's tiny feet are crossed, basking in the warm sunshine on his toes.

There was a time when I thought I would never come back here. It was too haunting, too raw; the trail had lost its magic.

As the bruises on my knees began to heal, I confessed what happened to a few friends. Without a single judgment, my fellow mother warriors offered me a surprising gift: empathy. One by one they each whispered their own confessions—tales of babies falling off beds, toddlers accidentally slipping down the stairs, scary moments in swimming pools, a night of co-sleeping that almost ended tragically. There were mothers all around me who could recall their own Worst Day in an instant. As much as I cringed hearing their stories, I took refuge in knowing I wasn't alone.

"Mommy do you see that?"

I follow Everett's little finger and look up to see a white streak of clouds in the sky, arching over the trail.

"It's like a cloud rainbow!"

I stare at the sky for a minute, suddenly feeling like Noah looking at a promise.

You are more than your worst day.

You are more than your biggest mistake.

I promise, this will not define you.

I push the stroller toward the cloud rainbow, my hands firm on the handlebar with the promise of grace floating right above us in the sky.

YOU ARE MORE THAN YOUR *worst* DAY.

YOU ARE MORE THAN YOUR *biggest* MISTAKE.

17

I'M GONNA NEED BACKUP

by Anna Jordan

I have a confession to make. Sometimes I fantasize about my husband dying. Not like I actually *want* him to die. I don't. My husband is wonderful. But how awful would it be if he did die? Several times a week he drives down to Los Angeles as the sun comes up, and then returns home to Santa Barbara late into the night. It's usually dark when he's on the road, and I know he's tired. He listens to books and podcasts and drinks lots of coffee, but still I constantly fear for his life. When I was pregnant with our third baby, I decided that instead of lying in bed at night, feeling my baby kick, wracked with worry that I may have to continue my motherhood journey alone, I needed a backup plan. In the wake of my husband's sudden vehicular death, my vision is this: channel grief into a riveting bestselling novel, meet Trevor Noah and have him fall in love with me, get married. In my imaginary widowed state, this plan is absolutely feasible. Also, I think every woman is entitled to at least one celebrity backup husband: Trevor Noah is mine.

After spending five long years grieving my deceased husband and penning emotional page turners, Trevor's South African sarcasm will be balm to my sad and weary soul. He'll woo me back to life with laughter. Also, my riveting best seller will be one of his favorite books, and he'll promote the sequel like crazy on his show (this is *my* fantasy, remember). In this dream, we become the perfect family. I might even have a fourth baby for him—and I will be the ideal, natural-birthing Earth Mother. My oldest son will have both a black father and a new biracial sibling, and everything will be perfect.

That last part is the key, you know. If I were meeting with a therapist right now, I'm sure she would home in on that final phase of the fantasy. Obviously, I have some issues to work through (and fine, it's probably not super healthy to regularly think about my husband's potential death), but the real kicker is the bit about my son. I know that. I love Trevor Noah, I do, but my backup plan isn't formulated to include him just because I'm going to need an adorable substitute foot massager after my husband is gone. I know that entertaining this fantasy is helping me work through an area where I am deeply insecure.

You see, my husband and I began our family with adoption through foster care. Our social worker phoned me on a foggy Friday in September to tell me about a possible placement.

"We have a nine-week-old African American boy—" I said yes before she could finish her sentence. We met him two hours later.

He was wailing, but he was perfect.

"He's probably the cutest baby I've ever seen," I said to my husband later that night. "Right? Don't you think he's just the cutest baby?"

"He's pretty adorable," my husband replied. He doesn't relish in hyperbole and absolutes the way I do. "Pretty adorable" is about as cute as a baby can be in his book.

And our little boy was just as cute as can be. We got comments everywhere we went. People stopped me in practically every aisle of the grocery store to commend the cuteness of my baby. I could hardly leave the house without someone mentioning his adorableness . . . or his race.

Here's the thing about being an interracial mother/baby combo: no one ever lets you forget it.

Once when my son was about three months old, we were at a coffee shop. I was wearing him in a wrap, and he was sleeping sweetly on my chest. I had gotten my coffee and was stirring in some cream when an older man walked up to me. I stepped aside, assuming he needed to pick up his beverage, but instead he looked at me closely and said "You've got a baby on your chest."

"Yes," I said. "I do."

"It's a boy," he added.

"Yes," I said. My baby was wearing a little blue beanie at the time, so I wasn't surprised at this observation.

"And he's black." The old man nodded at my son.

"Yep," I added. "He is."

The old man grunted and walked away. The interaction was gruff and a little odd, but I wasn't entirely offended. There was really nothing to be offended by. It was simply an old man stating a series of facts about my baby and then walking away. But the moment gave me pause. This was the first time I felt unsure. Like maybe if I were also black the old man wouldn't have said anything to me at all. Like maybe if we matched, fewer people would comment. Maybe if we matched, fewer people would ask questions.

As I walked back to my car with my still-sleeping baby and cup of coffee, I grew more uncertain. On one hand, I felt thankful that my baby was so little that he didn't have to participate in such a strange interaction. I wasn't sure whether comments about our racial differences would be a point of concern for him. But what would happen when he was older? What if someone made a similar comment when he could understand? How would I handle that? What would I say? More importantly, how would my son feel?

On the other hand, I wondered if the facts or realities of his adoption—the fact that he doesn't have the privilege of looking like his parents, or the realities of how he came to us—would be more troubling than any incident with a stranger in a coffee shop. *Will these issues be the undercurrent of his life? Will they become the undercurrent of mine?* I began to wonder, and worry: would the facts be a bigger hurdle than the odd encounter with outsiders?

My son is now five, and I'm still wrestling with these concerns. The real confession here is not that I want a celebrity backup husband. The confession is that I routinely feel ill-equipped to parent my son. I worry that I won't be able to give him what he needs as he grows. I worry that he'll feel misunderstood or like he doesn't fit somehow, either in our family or out in the world. I worry that he'll wish he had another mother—who isn't me.

When we first met our son, he was in the home of a respite foster family who was caring for him while he waited for his placement with us. We arrived at the respite home shortly after the social worker. He was a perfect ten-pound baby in a much-too-big onesie, crying in a car seat that belonged to the county. I bent down and unbuckled him, praying that he would stop crying in my arms, but he didn't. I instantly loved him, but I didn't feel instantly prepared.

We all start out ill-equipped in terms of our mothering abilities. This feeling of unpreparedness is nearly synonymous with motherhood, no matter how our children come to us. The doctors lay a little baby on our chests in the hospital or the social worker places a screaming six-month-old in our arms, or we fly halfway across the world to meet a toddler and take him home, and all of a sudden we each become a mother. We snuggle our sweet children and love them completely, yet we have no idea what the road of parenting them will look like.

Before my husband and I began our foster-care process, people asked us if we were going to have biological children as well. At that point, we didn't know what our family would look like. We simply said, "We'll get the children we're supposed to have." I deeply believed that. Before I became a mother, I was unshakably certain that God would give me the children I was meant to parent—either for a season or forever. And I still believe that I'm parenting the kids God gave me.

I can see the way my children fit together so clearly. When I watch my son and my middle daughter speak to each other in growls because they've decided that they are lion cubs for the day, I know that God gave them to each other for a reason. Now my youngest is old enough to participate, and she often roars from her high chair in response to their play. They are uniquely qualified to be each other's siblings.

But sometimes it's hard for me to believe that I am uniquely qualified to be their mother. Most days I feel like I'm captain of a ship that is far too big for me to steer, and I need a guide. I need backup.

A few weeks ago, my son asked when he was going to get a match. I asked him what he meant, and he clarified, "In our family, everyone has a matching skin. I don't have a matching skin." I looked at him and struggled for words. "Just you wait, baby. There's a South African comedian waiting in the wings for you," seemed like a really inappropriate response. So instead I reached out. I pooled my real resources—the whole families that look like ours, the friends who match, the books we've read about skin and family. Conversations about race and culture are, and have been, part of the fabric of our family for years, and as I spoke with my son about the ways God made each of us, I noticed that I had gathered more support than I realized. On the hard days, I need Trevor Noah, but on the good days, I rest in the fact that I have access to all the backup I need.

DIAMETER 9 INCHES · 23 CMS
LEGEND
Int'l. Boundaries
State Boundaries
Other Boundaries
CITY POPULATIONS
Star Symbol Indicates Capital
Cities more than 500,000
Cities from 100,000 to 500,000
Cities less than 100,000
Shelf Ice
Made in U.S.A.
CENTRAL
AMERICA
COLOMBIA
ECUADOR
PERU
Tropic of Capricorn (most southerly vertical sun rays, December 22)
SOUTH
AMERICA
BRAZ
BOLIVIA
CHILE
ARGENTINA
E
A
N

I INSTANTLY *loved* MY SON, BUT I DIDN'T FEEL INSTANTLY *prepared*.

I don't think God has made me uniquely qualified to parent my children, but He has given me all that I need to ultimately be prepared. He's given me love. As a parent, love is the ace up my sleeve when times get tough. Love is what drives me to stay up late at night googling children's books that feature interracial families. Love propels me to seek out a therapist who looks like my son. Love propels me to find activities for my child that put me in the minority so that he can feel like he really belongs. In fact, the more I build up my community and reach out to resources, the more I'm exposed to moms who are seeking backup for their kids too.

I see moms laying down their love card all over the place, in all different ways. We interview schools and go gluten-free. We buy left-handed scissors and keep a few pouches of prune puree on hand just in case. We stay up late to refill humidifiers. We buy inhalers and carry EpiPens. We find books and read blogs and scour websites. We pray. Ultimately, we find the backup that our children need, that we need. We don't need to wait for a better, more qualified fantasy parent to swoop in and save the day. We use our love to care for our children right here, right now.

18

A BREAK IN THE CLOUDS

by Katie Blackburn

The words flew off my fingertips and into the Google search engine, almost as if someone else was writing them.

"Late talker."

"Two-year-old developmental milestones."

"Toddler zone-out episodes."

"Autism."

An hour later I'm convinced of two opposite conclusions:

One, my son is a healthy, *normal* late talker. And two, my son is facing a real developmental disorder, one that he won't simply grow out of.

How can these both be true?

My mind seems cloudy in moments like this, like the gray skies of the late March weather. I see my sweet boy, developing at his own pace, perfectly healthy and happy. Then I see him again, nonverbal, not always responsive, hitting his head when he is frustrated, and burying his beautiful green eyes in his hands when I push him too hard to speak.

I return to my search results and continue mining for answers. I'm looking for something. Something to prove me wrong . . . or maybe to prove me right? I just need *something*. A reliable source of information to confirm that everything is okay and our son is *normal*. I find a checklist and start making my way through it.

Two dozen or more words? No.

Eye contact? Yes. But sometimes no.

Animal sounds? "Hey, big guy. What does the snake say?"

A big grin and he responds with, "*Sssssssssss*."

A break in the clouds. Sunshine streams in. He's totally fine.

Ability to mimic sounds? "Hey, handsome boy. Say *ball*." I work hard to emphasize the *B* sound, showing him how my mouth moves. But nothing. He's not looking at me anymore. Perhaps it was only a glimpse of golden beams coming through the window.

It feels like I'm looking outside right now, waiting for the weather to make up its mind, or listening to the meteorologist say there's a good chance it will clear up, but everyone knows to lean on the forecast with a healthy dose of skepticism. All I can really do is wait: wait for his development, wait to learn what resources he may or may not need. People tell me that I'll learn a lot in this season, in these weeks and months of mental Ping-Pong, back and forth between "something is wrong" and "everything will be fine." And I believe them. I do. Each is a well-intentioned voice speaking from the wisdom of the other side of the wait. Still, I'd do anything not to have to wait.

I think about my son and the months of speech therapy, yielding no real results; the board books and the dozen times every morning we point out the dog, then the cat, then the bee; the determination to make him speak, to force his eyes to meet mine—and the realization hits that none of this is up to me. Deep down I know it never has been, but that understanding is terrible consolation.

I'm used to results, to following a formula and seeing success: study for the test, get a passing grade; follow the directions, arrive at your destination; *do this, and that will follow.* But motherhood is not that kind of work. We are given some general guidelines, but every child seems to come with his or her own set of invisible instructions. Part of my job is to follow those instructions without exactly understanding them. Parenting is trial and error. Two steps forward . . . redo the last step. And sometimes, in the midst of all of your effort, the clouds gather overhead and the rain begins to fall.

What I really want right now is sunshine. I want the words to flow easily for my little boy, to have funny conversations with him, for him to tell me that he wants yogurt and not be frustrated as I guess ten different things until I get to the answer he's been waiting for. I want him to sing in the car with us. I want him to say his sister's name. I want him to stand up for himself

EVERY CHILD SEEMS TO COME WITH HIS OR HER OWN SET OF *invisible* INSTRUCTIONS.

with a "no" instead of a pinch or a bite. I want others to stop asking how old he is and if he is always so quiet, and I want to stop feeling insecure about why they're asking these perfectly natural questions.

And then it catches me unexpectedly, the next break in the clouds. His sister falls off the ottoman and immediately starts crying, and I say, "Oh, buddy. Go give Sissy a kiss." *And he does*, as if it's a command he's been following forever. A sweet show of empathy, a kiss on the arm. *See*, I tell myself. *He understands more than he lets on*. "Hey, sweet boy. Can mommy have a kiss too?" And he grabs my neck and pulls my lips to his. *He is doing just fine*.

This is motherhood—unpredictable and beautiful at the same time.

This is motherhood—unpredictable and beautiful at the same time. We hope for sunshine, but learn quickly that the weather can change in a moment, so we ought to prepare for anything. We make more appointments, find good resources, pray and ask for prayer, have a good cry and then display total confidence; but mostly, we just wait. And even with the knowledge that it won't last forever—and that soon enough we will know what storm we may have to weather—this watching, assessing, and wondering is difficult. We want resolutions, but sometimes the answers are long coming, and other times there just aren't any, and we have to learn to live and thrive and find joy right there in the middle of the wait. So much of motherhood is waiting, but so much of motherhood is also hoping, believing, and loving the work right in front of us.

Just as the weather forecast isn't always predictable or what we planned for, motherhood might also change our plans in every way. But that doesn't have to change the kind of momma I am. Not when I have a God who never changes. The glory of our good, good Father shines bright in any weather. All we have to do is put on our rain jackets and go look for it.

19

WHEN LOVE FEELS HEAVY

by N'tima Preusser

I am at my friend's baby shower. We're sitting in a room deliberately adorned with hand-crafted blue and green baby decorations. There is a banner, balloons, cake. I am surrounded by women making lighthearted jokes about new parenthood, sleep deprivation, and pregnancy cravings. I hear exchanges of favorite swaddle blankets and butt creams. But underneath the small talk and *oohing* and *ahhing* over tiny gifted baby clothes, sits the realness, the hardness, of motherhood. I can feel that every mom in the room, behind the gutters of her chronically sleep-deprived eyes, knows what that means. Each one has felt that weight. But they only have the heart to give gifts and hugs and congratulations. I sit there quietly, when all I want to do is let the momma-to-be in on the secret that is the agony ever present in motherhood.

I want so badly to prepare her, somehow, for the wave that is about to wash over her.

I was there too, belly rounded with life, it seems like yesterday. I had the iPhone app, the "Welcome, Baby" books, the nursery that I had pinned on Pinterest. I had the pacifiers, the overpacked hospital bag, the pretty dresses my girl would probably never wear. We toured the hospital. I googled birth stories while rounding my hips on a yoga ball. And I learned all about how you breathe a baby out of your lady parts.

I wanted so badly to prepare her, somehow, for the wave that was about to wash over her.

I remember eating whole pineapples and choking down giant evening primrose oil pills by the handful to will my baby out of my uterus.

I was ready.

I waited forty-two weeks and one day for her to arrive. Those extra eight days made me extra prepared. I remember sitting, ecstatic, in the hospital, after the epidural had been administered. I was too giddy to sleep. I was so ready.

Then in a blink, she was here. She was tiny and marveling. She was incredibly beautiful. She was perfect.

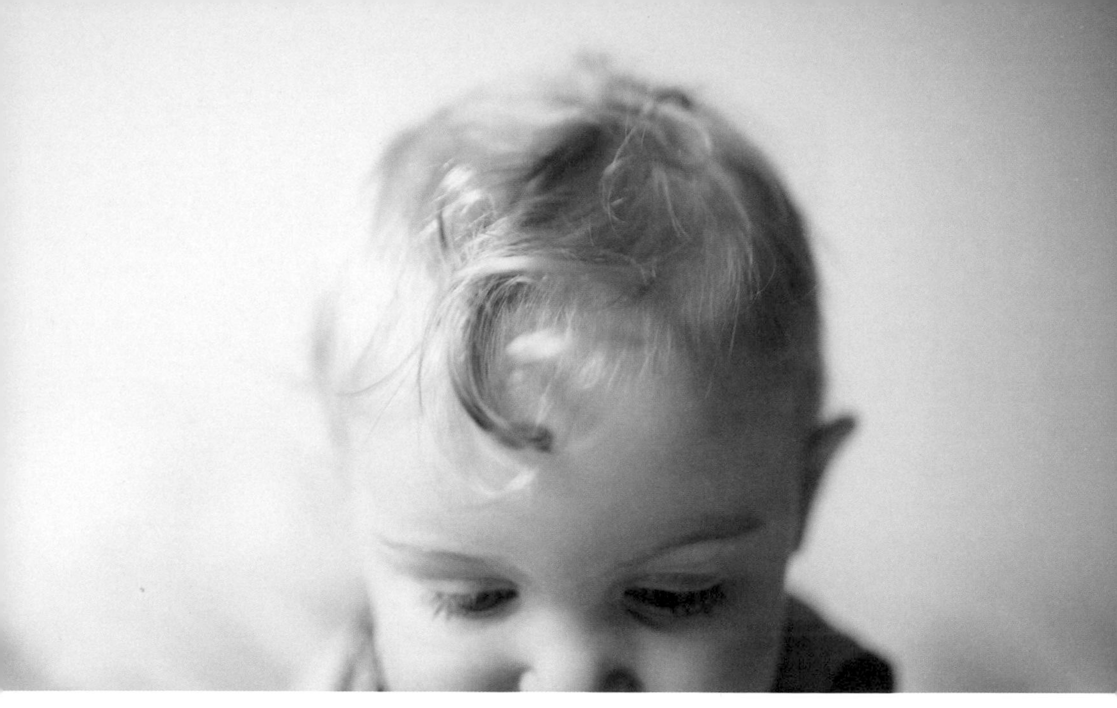

But wait.

I am not ready.

This is so hard.

I am so tired.

Why hasn't anyone prepared me for this?

I. Know. Nothing.

If I were sitting across from that very pregnant, very eager and innocent version of myself, I would grab her hands in mine and tell her this:

The love you will feel will be nothing like you have felt before. It will be foreign and familiar all at once. It will fill you to the very top of your heart, nearly spilling over. The thing about this kind of love, though, is that it can feel heavy. Disproportional. You may feel like you will nearly break in half from the top-heaviness. You will not be able to tell the difference between exhaustion and depression, and that darkness will rob you from what should be the most tender months of your daughter's new life.

Your baby will cry. A lot. Your days will both begin and end with the saddest screams you will ever hear. Your body will respond the way that it is programmed to—with panic. You will google everything from "dissecting baby poo" to "newborn who hates life." And you will come up short. You will always come up short.

Your baby will only sleep in ten-minute increments. In the bathroom. With the water running. You will feel like you are going mad, day after day, alone in that bathroom. Between the sound of the water and her screams, you may feel like your nerve endings will be permanently frayed.

After the endless ER trips you take, you will be written off as "the Paranoid New Mom." (Press on.) They will give you pamphlets on colic, and that will just not cut it. For a while, nursing will be excruciating, and your baby will fight it, hard. Contrary to the laws of nature, your baby will not come out knowing how to siphon milk from your body. Breastfeeding-induced anxiety attacks are a thing, and they will happen to you. (Hormones are jerks.)

Did I mention how depleted you will feel?

Eating, and sleeping, and showering are not a part of this season (not often anyway), and right now, in the thick of it, this season will feel never-ending. While others' newborns are napping sweetly on Instagram in their stylish organic leggings, yours is miserable. There are more than two billion mothers in the world, yet you will feel deeply alone. Compared to everyone else, you will feel you are failing.

This love will crush your ego. It will destroy your capability to trust yourself. The fear that creeps in the shadows of this love will paralyze you. Strangers will call your newborn "mean." Loved ones will say you are giving your baby too much attention. (Neither of those things exist.) You will feel guilty for not measuring up. You will feel guilty for feeling guilty. You will feel guilty for feeling guilty for feeling guilty. You will cry over absurd things, like not being pregnant anymore. And over massive things, like the way your body has transformed because of pregnancy. You may never feel like you will get the hang of carrying this love.

There will be a day when you will find a way to wrap that love around yourself instead of being buried in it.

But what if I told you that one day your daughter will smile? That she will even laugh? And so will you. Her intestines will eventually develop and digest food, and she will not scream excessively anymore.

I would also tell you that it gets better. Oh, how it does. She will learn how to sleep and nurse. And she gets really great at both. I would tell you to find the hope in your daughter's eyes. As they lighten, so will that weight in your heart.

Though you may never have parenthood all figured out, there will be a day when you will find a way to wrap that love around yourself instead of being buried in it.

And though it is hard to believe, one day you will have a vivacious, smart, and unbelievably happy little girl. A girl who absolutely adores the world. And you will have clean hair and time to make breakfast for yourself in the morning.

You will.

Hold on to that truth. There will be a day that you will marvel over the fact that the girl in front of you is the same baby that was so unhappy before.

You will be better. You will grow. You will adjust, and settle, and adjust again. That is what motherhood is, I think. Finding ways through the good heartbreak to fit more love inside of you. You will learn how to balance the goodness with the heaviness.

And, I beg you, embrace that things will always feel unfinished. Let unfinished be okay. Let unfinished be enough.

And forget what you see on Instagram.

You are one heck of a mother.

20

BAD WORDS

by Melanie Dale

Maybe the worst thing about sending your kids out into the world is that they bring stuff back with them.

My kids bring home more than just moldy food and rumpled homework in their backpacks. The minute I put my kids on a bus and it came back and spit them out onto our street, they returned with a smorgasbord of cooties and flu and a working knowledge of Rihanna videos. And the words. All the words. I picture the kids sitting at recess with swear flash cards, grouped around the ringleader, going, "It's pronounced 'PEE-niss-hed.'"

The other day, my son shared what he was learning with all of us at the dinner table. "At school we say, 'Go fork yourself,'

instead of the f-word." I'm either proud of this innovation or horrified.

How quickly things change. The f-word goes from the letter of the day on *Sesame Street* to that other one faster than you can say *fahrvergnügen*.

I remember when the f-word was *fart*. My kids weren't allowed to say it, and we were so precious with our *toots* and *bums*. And then, sometime over the last couple years, they've grown up, learned all the words, and I spend my days trying to teach them about impulse control. Just because you know it doesn't mean you have to use it.

They bring home new words, and also vermin.

A few months ago, I found myself dashing out to buy a lice kit because of a call from the school nurse. I spent the afternoon combing through hair and dreaming of empty nesting. Pro tip: put the kibosh on hugging. Girls like to hug and smash their heads together, so now I send my daughter out the door with a reminder that air hugging is a valid lifestyle choice.

At one point during the delousing, she actually said, "Mom, you're happy this happened because now you get to play with my hair, and you like playing with my hair. This is a good thing for you." Yes. These were actual words that were spoken over a lice comb during a nit search-and-destroy mission.

Sure, baby. This is the highlight of my day.

My husband and I joked that certain things seem to run in families. One family we know gets the barfs constantly. Someone is always puking over there. It's inexplicable. How can there be that much vomit in one house? Another has fevers. There's always a fever, as if they're permanently suspended in a Jane Austen novel where someone has gone out in the rain. In Regency England, getting rained on always led to fever, which led to bloodletting and a somber priest.

For us, it's ringworm. I tend to refer to it like I do Voldemort. You-Know-What. The Fungus That Shall Not Be Named. One time I had ringworm for a year and a half, and I've never mentally recovered. It hopped from one part of my body to the next. I lived in a constant state of laundering and tubes of ointment. I kept telling myself, "It's just a rash," but really I knew it was the spawn of Satan trying to take me down.

I'm on high alert for You-Know-What. If a kid so much as

scratches a bug bite, I squirt cream all over the spot and scream at her to wash her hands every five minutes. I'm itching psychosomatically as I'm writing this. Between the f-word, the nit picking, and the You-Know-What, some days I want to move to a deserted island and homeschool. Or maybe just buy more sanitizing wipes.

The truth is, no matter how much we try, we can't always control what our kids are exposed to. We send them out and they're going to pick up new words and gestures and communicable diseases. And we will survive and laugh about it like all the dark family comedies where the kids come home for Christmas or a funeral and they're screwed up but still love each other. The kids'll be okay.

No matter how much we try, we can't always control what our kids are exposed to.

When I finally held my son after five years of trying everything to get pregnant and stay pregnant, I felt my fists clench. I wanted to keep him safe, to protect him at all costs and not let the world blemish his perfection. I made my own baby food and cloth diapered and sheltered and protected. I was vigilant.

And one day I looked down to discover him eating someone else's goldfish crackers off the floor at Chick-fil-A. Then when he was learning to pull up on things, I turned my back for a millisecond and he fell and sliced the corner of his eye. There's still a tiny scar. And one year we hosted a teenager from an eastern European orphanage who taught him to scream, "Funky beach!" Only it wasn't funky beach. But with her accent that's what it sounded like, and my son copied her every move. So the boy who wasn't allowed to watch *SpongeBob SquarePants* because I thought it was crass was running around our front yard screaming "FUNKY BEACH!" at the top of his lungs. And last week he told me to go fork myself.

He's exposed. The world is all over him, and last year my daughter got ringworm all over her eyelid. Words and worms spreading all over our souls and skins, our insides and outsides all rife with contagion.

I think back to my own childhood, a good one, and I remember seeing that ripped-out heart in *Indiana Jones and the Temple of Doom* and hiding under my covers in fear. One day, I came home from school in third grade and proudly flipped my mom the bird. "Look what I learned today!" The older neighbor boy told me what sex was long before my parents were ready to have that talk. And at school I learned of Madonna and what "Papa Don't Preach" was all about. We go out and we learn things besides our multiplication tables and social studies.

Last week we spent an entire dinner discussing the finer points of obscene gestures with the kids. What's okay and what's not. How the middle finger stays down at all times. And my kids have created a whole new sign language of insults that aren't traditionally bad but they know what they mean and can giggle behind our backs.

We have conversations like this:

Her: Mom, what's the c-word mean?

Him: THERE'S A C-WORD?! I want to know it!

Me: (*treading very carefully*) What c-word? Tell me what you know.

Her: I think it's . . . it's . . .

Me: (*getting nervous*)

Her: "Crap."

Me: (*relieved*) Another word for *poop*. So many poop words.

Them: (*dying laughing*)

Another mom and I were talking about our daughters heading into middle school and the rise of mean girls out to destroy our young. There are big things looming, things that aren't as funny as elementary school euphemisms and gestures. Things worse than vomit and cooties.

But I don't feel scared. Maybe I should. My fists that once clenched protectively are becoming open palms. When I think about sending my kids out, I see their whole lives, the good and the bad. I see the stuff they'll have to learn the hard way because I did. I see the places where I hope they'll make better decisions than I did. Life is getting trickier to navigate as they step into the world and discover all it has to offer.

"It's not stalking. It's parenting." I want this on a mug.

The other day my daughter and I were talking about LoJacking her cell phone for safety. She called us stalkers, and I said, "We're not stalkers; we're parents. You have this short amount of time where we are your safety net. We're here to help you navigate this world. You can use us as an excuse, and you can blame us when you need to, and you can let us help you figure out how to make good choices. In just a few years you'll have to do all of that on your own. You'll make decisions about where you go and what you say and do, and we won't know about any of it. You'll be on your own. So for now, we are your protection and help. We have your back."

"It's not stalking. It's parenting." I want this on a mug.

The truth is, I love my growing-up kids. They learn how to hit the toilet when they do bring home the barfs. They learn how to smear on their own rash cream. And slowly, some slower than others, they learn a little impulse control with their new vocabularies.

The world is going to get all over your child. It'll probably be sooner than you'd like, and it might take you by surprise. Whether it's a germ or a verb, your kid will get something you weren't expecting. It'll be okay. Someday our kids will come home for Christmas and we'll laugh about these days together. We'll tell the stories. This is the beginning of a great life filled with other people, and other people are wonderfully weird.

And to whoever gave my kids eyelid ringworm and head lice, we're sending something your way soon.

21

BLACKBIRD, FLY

by Callie R. Feyen

I once called an old lady a jerk. I mean, she was really old, but I was only about three feet away, so I know she heard me.

I was on the way to the gym when it happened. Back then, when I was relatively new at this momma gig, the gym was like my church. It was my sanctuary. I walked in exhausted and overwhelmed, and I walked out refreshed and confident.

Part of that had to do with science, I know. Endorphins, blood flow, increased heart rate, and all that. Part of it had to do with the instructor, who, for one glorious hour yelled, "You can do this! You're doing great! Keep it up!" While sweat dripped down my back, I imagined she was only talking to me, and I believed her. She brought out strength that I didn't know I had.

I feel a little pathetic admitting that I relied on a daily dose of approval and encouragement from this woman. But there it is. I went to the gym daily to hear I was doing okay, and I had no tolerance for anyone or anything that got in the way of my pursuit of this message.

The morning I called the old lady a jerk went like this: Hadley, who was two, walked outside with a portable potty seat around her neck. "I wearing a necklace," she proclaimed, brightly. Harper, who was about six months old, decided sleeping from midnight to 3:00 a.m. was stupid, and in my exhaustion, I left the house in slippers. So Hadley was accessorizing with a toilet, and I was prepared to run a thirteen-minute mile in grey-and-white booties with pom-poms dangling from my shins. We traveled back up the three flights of stairs to our condo to fix our wardrobe malfunctions, then started over. Needless to say, as I buckled the girls into their car seats, I was anxious.

That's when the old lady drove up behind my car and parked right smack-dab in the middle of the road, so that her side door was behind the rear end of my car. She turned off the car, got out, and started walking down the street at the quick clip of a turtle.

I was infuriated. The nerve of her to park where you're not supposed to park, and then just walk away.

"Excuse me!" I yelled from my window. She pivoted shakily and looked my way. "I can't get out with your car there!"

She turned herself slowly to survey the situation, then turned away from me and resumed walking. She lifted an arm and flicked her wrist, as if to brush me off. "You're fine," she yelled. "You have plenty of space."

I was aghast. What did this woman know about space and me being fine? How dare she?

That's when I called her a jerk. In front of my two daughters, I leaned on the car door, so my head was completely outside and slowly proclaimed, "You're a jerk," in one, long, satisfying exhale.

Then I rolled up my window and began to cry. I was not fine.

Seven years later, around Christmas, I am holding warrior pose in a darkened room at the gym. I hate yoga, but I'm here because of the teacher. In the past, she's showed me things about myself I didn't know, and today, I believe she'll do the same.

This woman who helped me become a better mother is also a mom. She has two girls, like me. One of her daughters is a student of mine. She is a seventh grader with long, chlorine-bleached, shiny-blond hair, teeny tiny handwriting, and bitten-off nails. She has a talent for writing, but she holds herself back with her perfectionism. But I can't force her to let it go. I wonder about the difficulty of becoming yourself in adolescence. I think maybe it is similar to navigating who you are when you become a mother. I think maybe what she needs to hear in this moment is that she's doing great, and that she should keep going.

"Good job," I tell her. "This is a good job. You're doing great." Every day my instructor's daughter walks into my classroom, I think of what her mother did for me. So I take what I have become, what I have inside me, and offer it to her daughter. I pass on the gift of encouragement.

As we go through yoga poses, "Blackbird" by the Beatles plays on the stereo. I love this song about a bird taking her broken wings and learning to fly. We don't know if the bird did something to cause her wings to break. We don't know if something outside her circumstances broke them. What we hear is the soft, sweet melody of a narrator telling her it doesn't matter how they broke. She has everything she needs to stretch herself wide and take flight.

I think back to the old lady I called a jerk. She stood and watched me, her mouth open in shock at what I'd just called her, while I reversed the car and drove away. She was right when she told me I had enough space to get my car out and get where I needed to go. I didn't believe her, though. I was too angry, too stressed, too afraid. I never saw her again, and to this day I feel sorry I couldn't apologize. I'm sorry I couldn't tell her that she was right, that I had plenty of space to get where I was going.

The yoga class moves to warrior II, and I don't understand why this pose makes me feel strong. I try not to analyze it too much and instead, enjoy feeling strong. When our lunges become deeper, and we tilt to the side with one arm in the air, and another toward the floor, I know the best way to stay in this position is to have my face lifted up, toward the ceiling. My body won't do that, though. I have to look at the mirrors and see myself holding a modified position. I also see my instructor. She smiles, says, "Good job. You're doing a great job." And I know she's talking only to me.

We are all broken. We can all learn to fly. Thank God for mothers who give us a chance and show us how it's done.

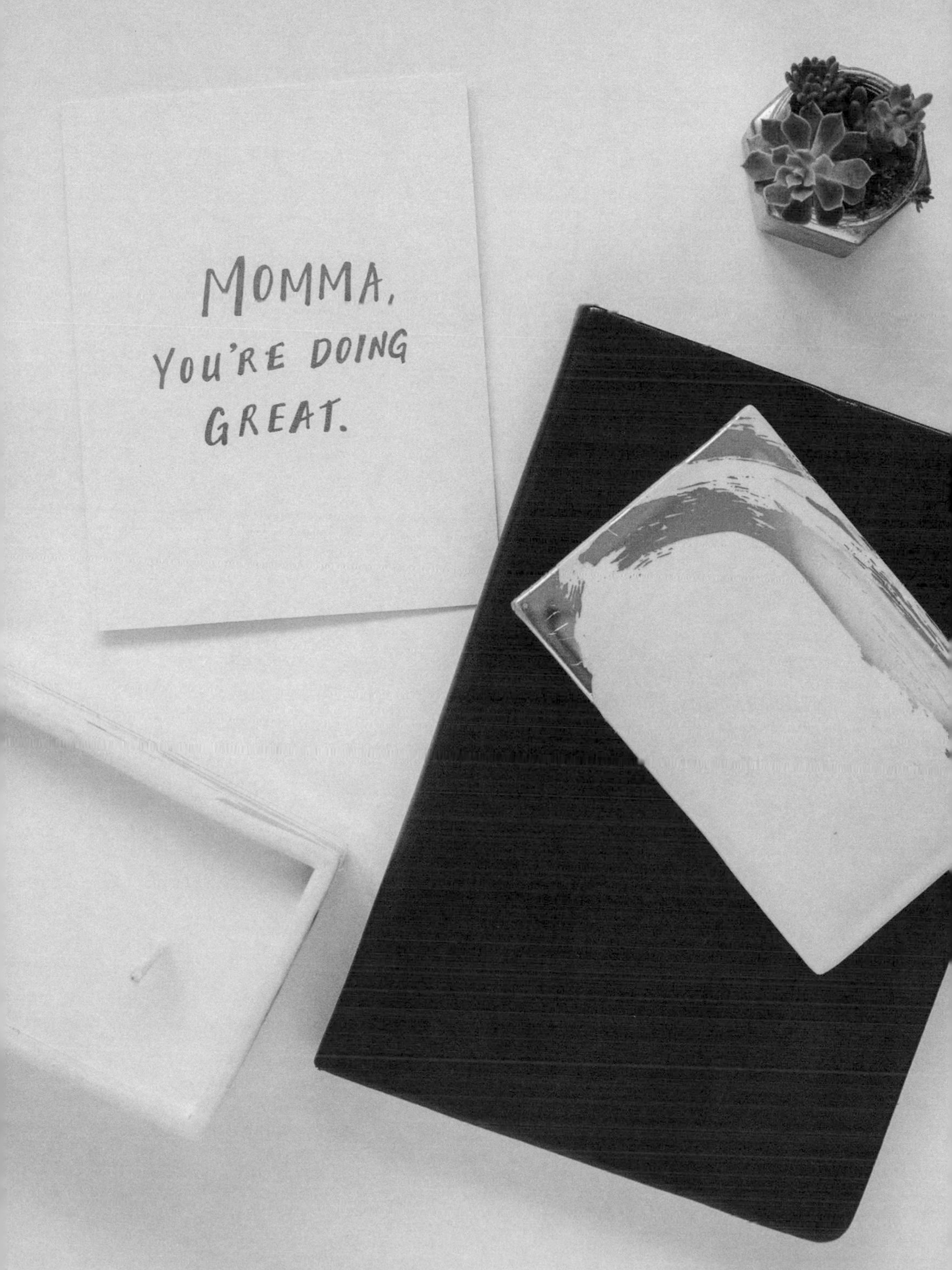
MOMMA,
YOU'RE DOING
GREAT.

22

CLIMBING MOUNTAINS

by Elena Krause

If someone were to ask how my husband and I knew it was time to start having kids, I would tell her that many years ago, on a Tuesday in April, it was like I'd discovered a giant hole in the floor of my house that I hadn't noticed before. Right in the middle of the living room—a hole so deep you couldn't see the bottom of it.

While walking from the kitchen to the front door that morning, it was as if I almost fell in. *Where did this come from?* I wondered, pressing my back against the wall. What was this?

This picture of the floor opening up in front of me is the best one I can think of to describe my first desire to be a mom—sudden, unexpected, startling. Inconvenient, even, because I couldn't just step around it and carry on; it demanded my full attention. This wasn't a sense of discontent or unhappiness; just a feeling like someone else should be here too. All I could think about was a squirming baby on my chest, tiny feet in my hand, the slight weight of a newborn in my arms. It was all I wanted in the world.

So that was the beginning. But having a baby is not as easy as realizing you want one, just as climbing a mountain is not as easy as deciding you're going to. And having a baby, in my experience, was a *lot* like climbing a mountain. Behind the chasm in the living room floor, the ground tilted steeply upward. I could not see the top—or anything past the first bend in the trail. This could be Mount Everest or a foothill, a dangerous expedition or an afternoon hike. I started the climb at once with all optimism, excitement, and love—and naivety. I had no idea.

A few months passed, then a few more. The atmosphere grew thin, and I became suspicious. This was taking longer than I thought it would, and I got tired before I thought I should. More months passed. I went from simply expecting that I would see the little pink plus sign each time I took a test, to hoping I would see it, to knowing I wouldn't.

I had a friend who'd been trying to conceive for almost ten years, and I watched her journey first with pity, then with dread, feeling like I was being granted a peek into my own future. When she cried in frustration, I wondered why she didn't give up. Then I realized that giving up was even harder than pressing on. A year passed, and then another one. I tried not to think about all the stories I'd heard of people who never made it to the top.

Around my two-year mark, it seemed like everyone else in the whole world became pregnant all at once. There was a rash of excited announcements, like falling dominoes: family, friends, acquaintances, strangers. Facebook posts, text messages, e-mails, phone calls. It wasn't a massive conception conspiracy; I was just at that age, and so were a lot of the people around me. I hugged them and congratulated them and tried so hard to feel genuinely happy for them. Then I went home and cried and felt like an awful person for crying, and then cried some more.

We kept it to ourselves at first. We didn't tell anyone about the hole in the floor or the hospital visits or the endless doctor appointments, procedures, or specialists. But then people started asking why we didn't have kids. Didn't we *want* kids? And when were we thinking we might start trying? So, out of resignation and some kind of self-preservation, I began admitting to everyone, starting with those closest to me, that yes, we were trying, but no, it didn't seem to be working.

It was surprisingly hard to explain to people why this was so difficult. Some liked to remind me that there was always a chance. That what I was going through was fairly common. That many people can't get pregnant right away. And that everything happens for a reason and I should enjoy my freedom and sleep now while I had it, and, and, and . . .

It was a kind of wound, one that was constantly being picked open. Like a cut on the bottom of my foot. How could I avoid thinking about it when every time I took a step, there it was? I couldn't stop walking, but the pain was awful. So I limped and winced and made halfhearted attempts to grin and bear it. I did not want constant pity—I wasn't sure I deserved it—but I didn't want to be forgotten either. I knew my friends loved me and wanted to help, but I didn't want to bother them too much—a hard balance to strike, especially over time.

But whether it showed on my face or not, I thought about it daily. Hourly. I thought about never being called Mom. No one to take care of. No grandbabies for my parents. Holidays and vacations, just the two of us. I thought about giving up, but then I thought about the hole in the floor and having to balance on the edge of it forever. I thought about being left behind as my friends and family all stepped into this new world without me, a world with a different vocabulary, a different schedule, a different list of priorities, a different everything.

I thought about not knowing what it was like to feel a baby kick inside my swollen belly.

Infertility is suspended grief for a funeral that hasn't happened yet. As the months tick by, the dream of motherhood lies on its deathbed and time races with alarming speed toward a day when all your chances are used up. But at some point, you start to feel awkward about it, like it should be old news and shouldn't bother you anymore. You hate being the infertile one, the one people feel they have to tiptoe around, the one who cries in the bathroom at baby showers after one too many insensitive comments—made by wonderful, well-meaning people who just don't know what you need. (How can they when *you* don't even know what you need?) And you hear about people who have been through much worse, people who have never gotten what they wanted. You're still young, there's still a chance, and you

INFERTILITY IS SUSPENDED *grief* FOR A FUNERAL THAT HASN'T HAPPENED YET.

have so much to be thankful for. So you feel embarrassment and even guilt.

A note for those still on this journey: I know it's hard, and I know it doesn't get easier. I wish I could guarantee you success, but all I can guarantee you is that you're not alone. Be okay with crying, and call it grief—it's legitimate. Don't feel guilty or embarrassed about it. Be honest with the people around you. Try to learn to share in their joy (this is a very valuable life skill) but don't be afraid to ask them to share in your pain too.

If I could go back a few years and tell myself only one thing, it wouldn't be that someday I would have a baby. It would be this: no matter how everything turns out, this time of wanting and waiting and hoping is so valuable. That's all. It's a life lesson for all stages, no matter if you're waiting for a baby, a partner, a job, or a train. This climb is exercise and experience. The view from halfway up the mountain can be beautiful too, when there's a break in the trees. This is an opportunity to grow, to learn, to experience joy that's not dependent on life circumstances. To experience relationships that are rich and honest. To experience the freedom in realizing how little control you actually have over your life.

My own experience with infertility ended on May 24, 2013, with a positive pregnancy test. I sat on my bed, but it felt like I was sitting on a mountain summit, looking down at where I had come from. The gaping hole in my living room floor was such a distant memory now. I was exhausted, and exhilarated, and completely in shock. Proud and humbled at the same time, knowing I had come a long way but knowing I hadn't done it alone.

I hadn't known when I started this climb how long it would take, or how hard it would be. Or how much I would learn and grow and be stretched and changed. Or how beautiful the view would be from up here. But as I sat there, I decided that this moment was well worth the journey. That's the thing about mountains, I guess. People wouldn't go through all that work to climb them if there wasn't the potential for something amazing at the end.

I put a hand on my belly and said, "Hello."

23

THE FAMILY BABY

by Lesley Miller

My mother-in-law loves babies. I learned this one Christmas when my husband and I announced my pregnancy. Ours would be the first grandbaby, and I think most of the family had been waiting since our wedding night for the news. In somewhat cliché fashion, we wrapped a framed ultrasound photo and placed it under the Christmas tree. Upon its opening she screamed. Her reaction was so sweet and very appropriate, but I wasn't prepared for what came next.

"The girls and I have been discussing when you'd get pregnant," she said, as if my uterus and sex life were something the family casually chatted about over coffee and pancakes. "I knew it was coming," she said.

I swallowed hard, forcing a smile. *I* hadn't really known it was coming.

I remember standing in the kitchen later that afternoon, during the quiet hour before dinner when everyone else was examining their presents and munching on artichoke dip. My mother-in-law effortlessly moved around the kitchen, wearing a holiday apron, chopping food and discussing summer travel plans. It was her birthday in August, a few weeks after the baby's due date, and the only thing she really wanted was for the entire family to vacation together.

Her eyes widened. "And to think, we'll have a baby with us by then!"

We.

We will have a baby.

Our whole family is having a baby.

The baby in your belly is ours.

The weight of our child's life suddenly hit me in a way it hadn't before. This baby—this mysterious grouping of cells with a heartbeat and arm buds—wasn't just mine. We'd created a person, and our temporary secret was now available for our families to discuss, long for, and lay claim to. It was our baby to name, but they could offer opinions about which options sounded too formal, too outdated, too modern, too odd. It was our baby to raise, but they might offer their thoughts on pacifiers and sleep training. It was our baby to welcome into the world but they'd be waiting right outside the delivery room doors, eager for our bonding time to end so theirs could begin.

But to be honest, the delivery room was the least of my

AT ITS BEST, THIS *love* FELT COMFORTING AND HOPEFUL, A PROMISE RELEASING US, THE TERRIFIED NEW PARENTS, FROM BEING HER EVERYTHING.

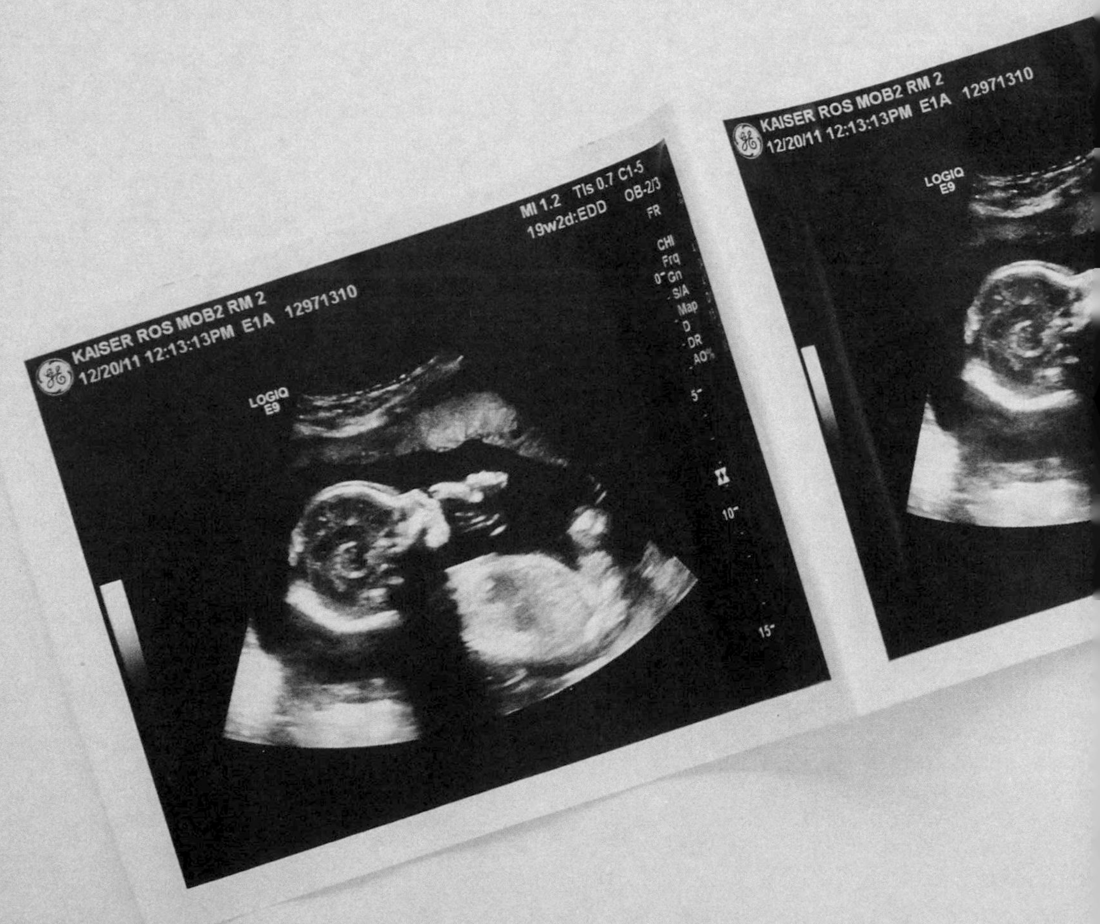

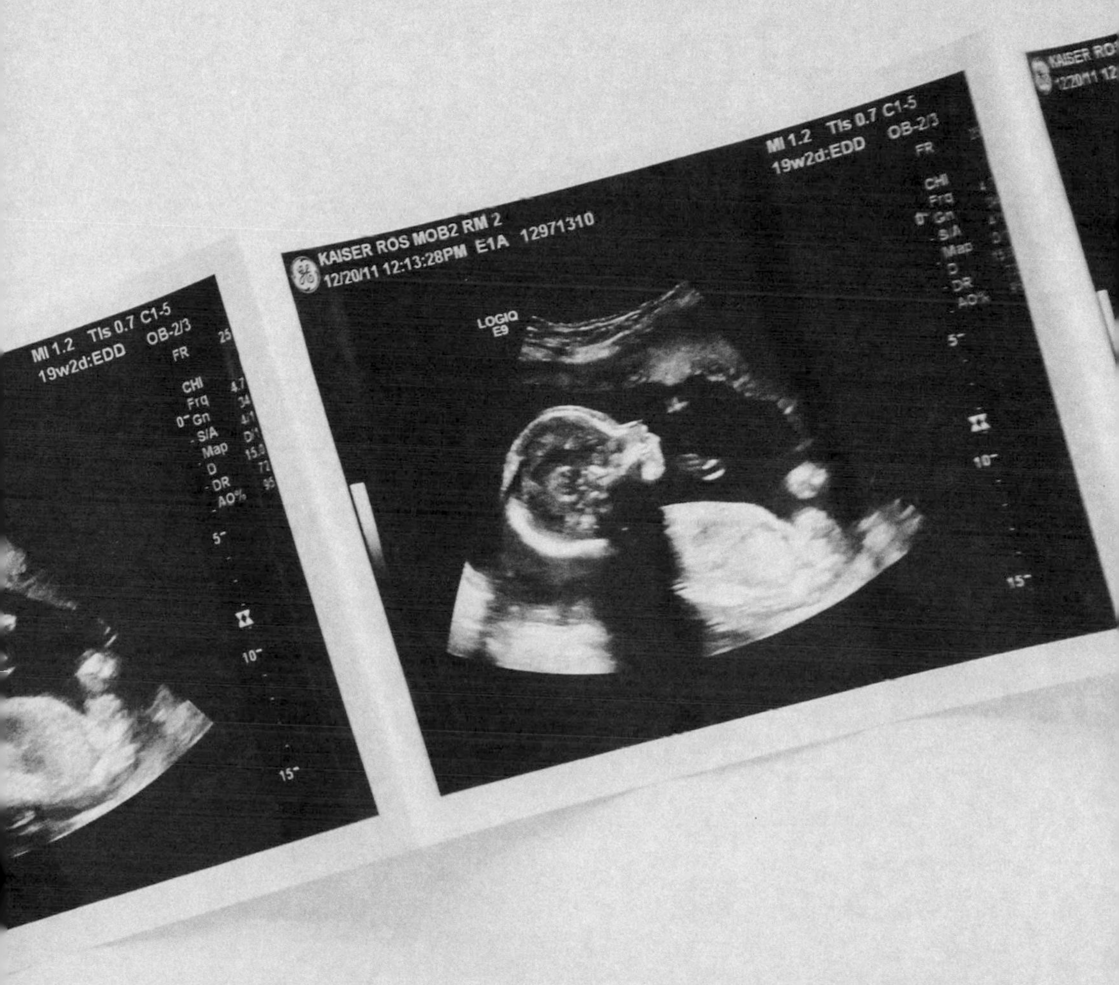
MI 1.2 TIs 0.7 C1-5
19w2d:EDD OB-2/3
FR
CHI
Frq
Gn
S/A
Map
D
DR
AO%
5
10
15
KAISER ROS MOB2 RM 2
12/20/11 12:13:28PM E1A 12971310
MI 1.2 TIs 0.7 C1-5
19w2d:EDD OB-2/3
FR
CHI
Frq
Gn
S/A
Map
D
DR
AO%
LOGIQ
E9
5
10
15

worries at that point. I was only thinking about how my heart hadn't stopped racing since the positive pregnancy test, and how I was going to tell my boss the news, and whether I wanted to return to work full time, and what this was all going to cost, and if this baby would even make it to the forty-week mark. There are no guarantees, after all. My pregnancy was wonderful news, but it was already affecting my life dramatically. Crammed against my ribs, forced between my stomach and spleen, this baby felt like an extension of myself. How could it belong to anyone else?

As the months went by, and we got closer to her due date, my husband and I began having conversations about what the first moments of her life would look like. Did we want family in the delivery room? When would it be okay for them to visit in the hospital? Would I feel up for visitors? Would it be awkward to have my dad or brother-in-law see me in a breezy hospital gown? And how should we decide which family would hold the baby first—my parents, or his? In retrospect, these questions seem silly, but at the time they felt like a very, very big deal. Everyone wanted a phone call when I went into labor, and everyone planned to arrive as soon as she was born. Now, years later, their love is so evident. At the time though, it felt very overwhelming.

I remember those early hours of her life, when she was no longer nestled under my heart but resting in my arms. The nurse wheeled us to a postpartum room, and within a half hour we had visitors. It was eight in the morning, and the breakfast cart hadn't even arrived. Feeling a mixture of reluctance and pride, my momma-bear hormones surging, I passed her off to waiting aunties, uncles, and grandparents. My mother said she looked just like my husband, while my mother-in-law insisted the baby was a spitting image of my dad. We all looked for ourselves and each other in her face. *She is ours. She is ours. She is ours,* we said in subtle ways.

And I guess that's part of motherhood no one prepared me for—something that starts as an intimate act between husband and wife soon becomes a love extending much further and deeper. To be honest, such love took getting used to. In the beginning, and at its worst, this love felt competitive and possessive. In those early weeks I wanted the baby close to me at all times, and I felt reluctant every time a grandma or auntie insisted I nap while they held her. It seemed everyone wanted private bonding moments, but I didn't feel like sharing. Did I have to?

But at its best, this love felt comforting and hopeful, a promise releasing us, the terrified new parents, from being her everything. Because we soon found that we could never fill such a role on our own, nor would we want to. Raising her is a huge responsibility, and the more people willing to help, the better. In her baby days, holding her was all anyone could do, but as she grew we started to see that each aunt and grandma, uncle and grandpa, could play a unique role in creating a rich life of meaning and memories. One day, perhaps, she'd even create special traditions with each of them, similar to how my own grandmother took me shopping every year on my birthday, and my aunt Debbie made Christmas cookies with me each December. The greatest lesson we can all teach our daughter is that she is not simply an extension of her mother and father, but a girl created by God with deep purpose, unique gifts, and a capacity to love and be loved beyond the confines of our nuclear family.

Someday, I hope, my sweet girl will have her own children. These days she says she wants to be a mommy when she grows up, and I often ask her if I can help with her babies. It's as if I already can't help myself. I'm already loving a baby that is years and years away from existing on this earth. Love is incomprehensible like that. I hope I can be the type of mom who paces patiently in the waiting room until she calls for me, just like our families did for us, but I'm fairly certain that at some point I will tell her baby, "You look just like your momma, and I can't wait for her to fall asleep so we can bond."

Our sweet newborn is now five, tall like me with long eyelashes just like my husband. Her thin frame reminds me of her aunties, and her big feet are mine. She also loves to bake, just like her grandma. I believe that her kindness, curiosity, and joyful spirit are learned traits from all of us. She doesn't like to be held much anymore, but with time, we've all realized we didn't need to hold her so close to begin with. Because she is the daughter of the King—not ours to own, but all of ours to love.

24

MOMMY HAS TWO ARMS

by Anna Jordan

"Did you play a dominant-armed sport in college?" the chiropractor asked. I was seated on the table as she worked her hands between my right shoulder blade and ribs. She lifted my arm up to my ear and pressed her fingers between my shoulder and collarbone.

"No," I said.

"Hmm," she replied, moving my right arm up and down in a slow, rhythmic motion. "You didn't play volleyball? Tennis?"

"No." I shook my head. My injury occurred this week, not twelve years ago. I couldn't figure out why she was asking me these questions.

"You have significant strain on your rotator cuff, particularly on the right side. It's just—breathe out—" she popped two of my ribs back into place—"I typically see this kind of wear and tear on athletes who played a competitive dominant-armed sport at the college level."

I tried to laugh through my pain. "Oh, well, if that's the case, my sport is motherhood."

"Ha! I should have known," she said as she gently laid me facedown on the table. "This makes sense with the tension I feel on your left side." *Pop.*

"Co-sleeping with the baby in the crook of your left arm . . . hmm . . . that's right here." *Crack. Pop.*

"Breastfeeding can really throw off alignment in your neck." *Pop. Pop.*

"You should probably try to carry your kids on your left side more to balance out this strain." *Crack. Crack. Crack.*

I had thrown out my back just the day before. My middle daughter, Vivienne, had her annual parent-teacher conference at the preschool. With my husband out of town and my sitter unavailable, I had no choice but to bring both Vivi and my youngest, Eloise, with me to the meeting. As is typical for any kind of excursion with my girls, I packed as though we were venturing out on a week-long safari: sippy cups, packages of Puffs, several cereal bars, a snack stack container of blueberries and snap peas, diapers, wipes, some picture books, and—most importantly—six Little People Disney Princesses in their corresponding blue satin Disney Princess purse. I tossed everything into my diaper bag and strapped my daughters into their car seats.

As I drove to the conference, I noticed that my neck felt a little stiff. I did a few shoulder rolls at a stoplight and assumed I'd feel better as the day wore on. I usually did.

I felt decidedly uncomfortable as we slowly stepped down the stairs to the preschool director's office. Why is it that children run everywhere but then navigate stairs at a snail's pace? When we finally sat down in the desk chair at the parent-teacher conference, I leaned forward to place the baby on the ground and set my beastly bag next to her. When I sat up, my back seized. I could barely move. Frozen with pain, I did the only thing I could do: I smiled and continued that parent-teacher conference.

Before becoming a mother, I had anticipated the emotional strain of motherhood. We adopted our oldest, Mason, through

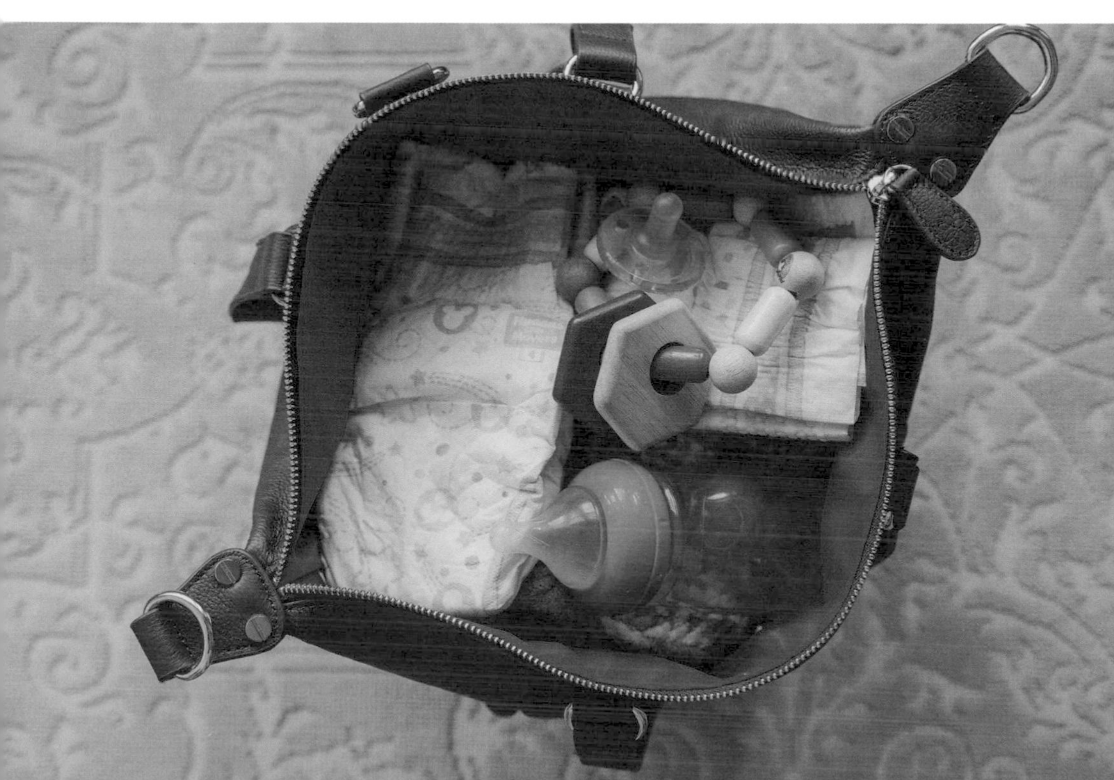

the foster system, and I had taken all the classes and read all the books. We spent a substantial amount of time with our social worker discussing the complexity of bonding with a child who had experienced trauma. I felt as mentally prepared as I could to receive that placement call. But the truth is, I wasn't prepared. I couldn't anticipate the pain and stress of visits with birth parents. I didn't expect all the paperwork and record keeping. I didn't have the supplies to change a diaper or even give a bottle. But more than all that, I wasn't prepared for this tiny little person to capture my heart. I was simultaneously surprised by how much he needed from me and how much I was able to give and keep giving.

Mason was placed with us on a Friday afternoon at 1:25 p.m. as I was coming out of a hot yoga class. Just the week before I had started training for my second half marathon. Any aches and pains I felt at that point were purely my own.

However, in those first few weeks and months of motherhood, my body grew tired under the weight of this growing baby boy. I wore him in a baby carrier, napped him in a sling. My back ached and my arms grew stronger.

When I became pregnant with Vivienne, I experienced another significant physical transformation as my body made room to accommodate more life. From my hair to my feet, everything changed. A woman's body can do amazing things, but not until after the birth of my daughter did I discover my true athletic prowess.

Vivi was born on a Wednesday at 3:33 a.m. We were released to go home from the hospital on Friday. My husband was back at work by eight Monday morning. By noon on Monday, I had accomplished more than I ever thought humanly possible. Wiping a toddler booty while nursing an infant? Check. Making a peanut butter sandwich while nursing an infant? Check. Changing a diaper with a two-year-old climbing up my back? Mission accomplished. I was a one-woman feeding, cleaning jungle gym. There was nothing I couldn't do.

I tried to laugh through my pain. "Oh, well, if that's the case, my sport is motherhood."

And so it continued.

Over the past couple of years, perhaps I've built in my children too much confidence in my abilities. Over time, their requests have become more outlandish. Now, no matter how much I try, I find myself unable to accommodate all their demands. So I've begun to voice my limitations more clearly.

"I can't lift you and separately carry your shoes while I'm also carrying two bags of groceries. Sorry, babe. Mommy only has two arms."

"You need me to put Elsa's dress back on while holding your sister and stirring a pot of chicken soup? Hey, girl. Mommy only has two arms."

"Believe it or not, I actually am not able to make a turkey sandwich while assembling a Duplo structure. Mommy only has two arms."

My children are understandably disappointed with the limits

of my limbs. They're children: their job is to ask for the impossible. Yet I am also often dismayed by my own limits. Sometimes I feel like I'm at capacity before we've even finished breakfast. I can never make eggs, kiss owies, and pour a cup of coffee while also remembering where Dusty Crophopper is as fast or as seamlessly as I hope. Still, I spend my days lifting, hugging, diapering, and snuggling my three sweet appendages. If my body is telling me anything, it's that these two arms have been working awfully hard. They've been put to good use, and where I may think I'm at capacity, my body is actually incredibly capable.

As the chiropractor worked her way through my upper back, cracking and popping and realigning everything from my spine to my knuckles, I couldn't help but feel thankful. I was in pain, yes, but it was the good kind of pain. It was the pain that comes from accomplishing great feats; the pain that comes from giving all you've got and then digging deeper for more. Like the college athlete my chiropractor thought I was, I have done some good, defining work with these two arms. In fact, more than I ever imagined. And I have so much more ahead of me.

25

STILL US

by Ashlee Gadd

It's 3:26 a.m., and the baby is crying. Again. You're sleeping soundly next to me, your chest rising up and down ever so slightly with each breath. Moonlight shines through the window, casting a faint glow over your peaceful head.

I want to punch you in the face a little bit.

I settle for your arm.

"I got up last time. It's your turn," I say coldly.

You grunt in response. The baby cries on.

We continue this dance for a few more minutes: I poke your body, you grunt, I complain, repeat. Eventually our whispers turn to attacks, and then to comparisons of the most ridiculous kind. Next thing I know, we're arguing over who needs more sleep, whose job is harder, whose daily responsibilities will suffer more as a by-product of inadequate rest. And so on.

Nobody ever wins an argument at 3:26 a.m. We know this. We go to bed with our backs turned.

I close my eyes and remember a pillow someone gifted us at our engagement party. It said "love" on the front and everyone wrote down their best marital advice with a sharpie pen on the back.

One of the lines read: *Don't ever go to bed angry.*

What a bunch of crap.

+ + +

The night before we became parents, I was standing in the doorway of our bathroom with a toothbrush in my mouth when the realization hit me.

This is our last night as a family of two.

After months of decorating a nursery and feeling a tiny human doing somersaults in my belly, you'd think I'd be used to the idea. Somehow I had made peace with most of the other shifts: my changing body, a house suddenly filled with baby gear, a new lifelong commitment that would alter my identity and heart, not to mention my daily schedule and still-evolving career.

But our marriage? Unintentionally, I had saved the processing of that change for the very last minute: 10:00 p.m. the night before the scheduled C-section, to be exact.

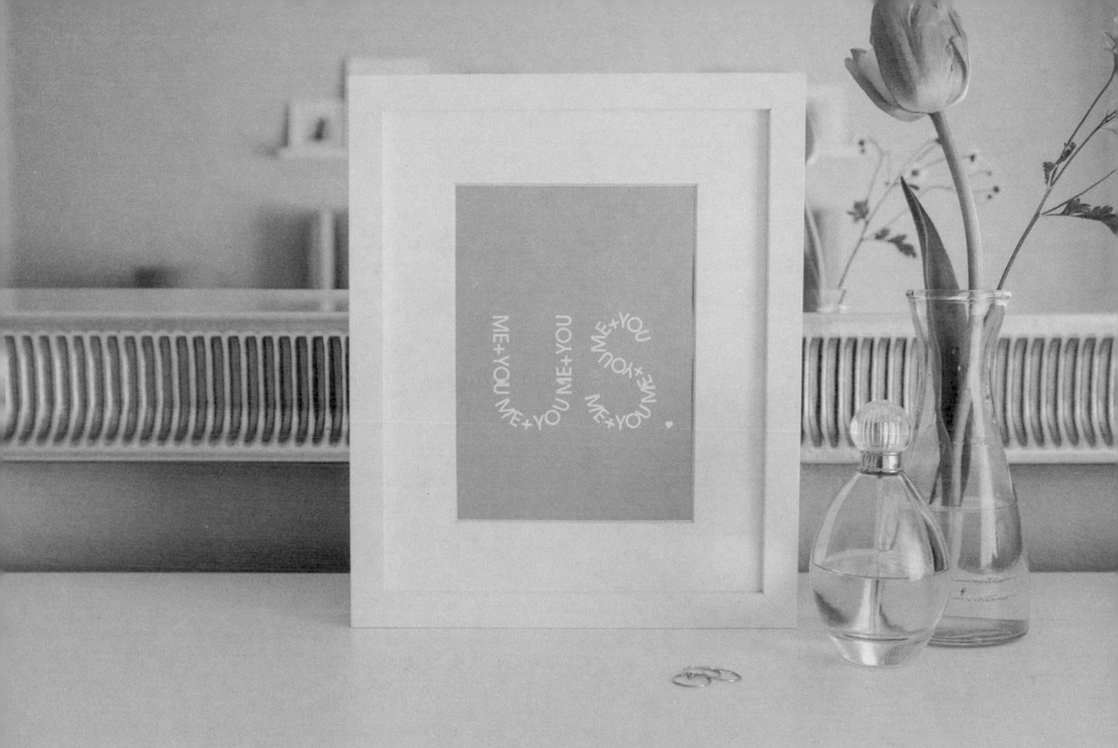

A wave of panic washed over me and I began sobbing, my mouth full of toothpaste.

You rushed to my side, worried. "What is it? Are you okay?"

I managed to choke out bits and pieces of the emotions unraveling in my mind: how scared I was, how bittersweet that night felt, how much I was going to miss the pre-kid version of us.

You wrapped your arms around me and smiled.

"We'll be okay," you promised.

I wanted to believe you, but my heart remained a weird mixture of terrified and paranoid. I had so many fears, so many questions. Would our marriage end up on the back burner? What if the flame burned out? How would we protect it?

In that moment of panic, I was so focused on what our marriage was giving up that I didn't even have time to think about everything it would gain.

+ + +

Do you remember New Year's Day 2006, before we were married, when I woke up writhing in pain and my mom called you from the car?

I was so focused on what our marriage was giving up that I didn't even have time to think about everything it would gain.

"We're taking Ashlee to the emergency room. You can meet us there," she said.

Somehow you beat us to the hospital. You showed up in your pajamas, hair all awry, not an ounce of caffeine in your blood. An hour later, I was hooked up to a morphine drip, sweet relief running through my body while the doctor muttered something about a kidney stone. The morphine made me sick, and I started puking in a bucket right in front of you, my adorable boyfriend who had barely seen me without makeup. I was mortified. You never even flinched. I stayed in that hospital bed all day while you held my hand in yours.

Six and a half years later, we took up residence in a different hospital room. I was watching you hold our newborn baby while the pain meds crept through my veins and made me nauseated. In a matter of seconds, you handed the baby off, grabbed a bin, and shoved it right under my face while I got sick. Our baby was barely two hours old, still fresh and new and a miracle to hold, but you sprang into action without a second thought. Someone else held our baby while you held back my hair. For as long as I live, I will never forget that—in your first few hours as a dad, you still chose me.

Four years into parenthood, our marriage has grown and stretched, sometimes against its will, like a too-small T-shirt being pulled over my head. Some days it feels like the old version of us is a ghost, floating around the house, taunting us in superiority. Other days I like the new version of us better—no doubt these kids have made us stronger, closer, and more resourceful.

But my favorite days are when the two worlds collide, when a bit of the past meets a moment of the present and all of a sudden I'm recognizing a piece of my old life inside my new one.

Once upon a time, our weekends were lazy. We used to lounge on the couch in our sweats all morning with our legs entangled, a pretzel of limbs. I made you breakfast; you rubbed my feet. My coffee stayed hot and your energy drink stayed cold. We had all the time in the world.

Now we're up at 6:00 a.m. on Saturdays with the same routine as weekdays—cartoons on the TV and two cups of Cheerios being spilled on the couch while you and I drink coffee with our eyes closed. Our weekends are full and exhausting from dawn till dusk. Downtime looks like lying on the floor while children climb on our backs, running toy trains down our legs, pretending we're human railroads. And there, on the carpet, our bodies melting lazily into the ground, I see it. You smile at me and I smile back. We're still us.

Once upon a time, our love was sustained through big romantic gestures—surprises and gifts, rose petals and love notes. You made me dinner and lit every candle in the house. I surprised you on your birthday with breakfast in bed and plane tickets for a spontaneous getaway. "We leave in an hour! Pack your bag!" I ordered with a mischievous grin.

My favorite days are when the two worlds collide, and all of a sudden I'm recognizing a piece of my old life inside my new one.

Oh, the romance back then. I remember it well: the lingerie, the slow dancing in the kitchen.

Let's be honest: I miss it sometimes.

You probably do too (mostly the lingerie).

And yet.

Last week you put gas in my tank because you noticed it was almost empty, and I know you do that because you love me. I have to look extra hard to see all the little ways we love each other now. It's in the last of the milk that you left for me, and in the four-dollar bouquet of flowers you brought home from Trader Joe's. It's in the peanut butter cups I snuck into the cart for you, and in the way I fold your T-shirts. Every once in a blue moon, you surprise me with a grand gesture, like the time we sat at dinner celebrating my small writing victory and you handed me a poem that *you* (the nonwriter) had written for me that afternoon. I cried all over my meatballs, and there it was again. We're still us.

In some ways, everything is smaller now, but when I think of the effort it takes to love each other amid a year's worth of sleep deprivation and fifty-six days of potty training and all of the other exhausting situations we find ourselves in . . . there's really nothing small about it.

Underneath all the chaos, the celebration and grief, the leaking sippy cups and mushy fruit snacks between the couch cushions, *we* are still there. I can still see *us*, the love that founded and grounded all of it.

It's morning. There are dishes in the sink from last night's dinner, but the kitchen smells like coffee and forgiveness. You grab my favorite white mug, the large one, and add the perfect amount of hazelnut creamer before sliding it toward me on the counter.

A peace offering.

We're too tired to apologize with words, so we apologize with our eyes. We're both sorry, we know. Fighting at 3:00 a.m. is dumb. We're tired. It's okay.

If anything, I'm reminded that marriage has been, and continues to be, a refining process.

Sure, it's only a cup of coffee you're offering me, but it's more than that. This coffee is everything: a fresh start, a reminder that every day we wake up and make the choice to stay, to put in the work, to lay down our own selfish desires for the good of the other person, for the good of this marriage and for the good of this family.

While we may not be the same couple we were twelve years ago (skinny, tan), or even five years ago (two disposable incomes), or even four hours ago (zombies), when I look into your eyes after a long night of broken sleep, I know there's nobody else I'd rather do this holy work of raising children with than you.

Because I love you. And you love me. And underneath it all, we're still us.

26

ANXIOUS

by N'tima Preusser

The electrocardiogram showed a lively pulse.

"My chest feels tight."

My ribs fold into themselves in a braidlike motion toward a limited amount of space. My bones are tightening their grip until my lungs are deflating. There is a loaf of challah rising in my chest. There isn't space to breathe here.

"I get lightheaded sometimes."

My muscles and bones are detaching from my skin. My nervous system doesn't feel connected anymore, and my head gets wobbly.

"I think I have a heart condition."

I have already diagnosed myself.

The doctor talks to me like I am a child. He uses the words *healthy, normal, flawless, strong*. His hands are drawing pictures in the air to make things plainer for me. I imagine he's seen people like me before. In the end, I leave with my demons on paper, hashed out in bold print: "Living with Anxiety."

It is the same old story. I am anxious, and I am sure I always have been. I picture myself in my mother's womb, agonizing over my very own entrance into the world. My body has never known when it is supposed to be nervous. A part of me wished an organ was failing so I would have something tangible to blame. I can tell you the exact moment it began to haunt me, the very moment I felt abandoned for the first time. And that single incident was enough to persuade the chemicals in my brain to shift right into the place in which they were created to live: unbalanced.

I was nine years old when I talked to the man, the shrink, behind the desk for the first time. He would shout across the room at me to make me battle my fears. He would pretend to be angry with me, furious, even, so I could retrain my mind to not dissolve in fear if it were to really happen with the people I encountered daily. I remember round salmon-colored pills I took in the nurse's office each day to help balance the serotonin levels in my brain. I remember the panic attacks that would paralyze me before school. And I remember my teachers turning into monsters; it was as if they breathed fire. I was constantly afraid that everyone was going to hurt me.

+ + +

Now I am a mother. And being a mother with mental illness is an art of balance in which I am always dizzy. My feet never feel planted into the ground. It so often means that I have to hold what is devouring me on the inside, destroying me even more. It means constantly trying to decipher the difference between normal "mother's intuition" and plain old paranoia.

Am I the only one who harrows over every mistake?

Does every mom prop her newborn in a specific position that will prevent suffocation in the night? Do they hold their toddlers' hands with a grip as tight as a handcuff while they are walking in a parking lot together? Am I the only one that leaves the baby monitor on, blaring and bright in the dark so as to not miss a single exhale that leaves my babies' lips? Am I the only one who doesn't know if I am supposed to catch them or let them fall? Am I the only one who harrows over every mistake?

Am I the only one?

Then there's a blurry line of in-between, where motherhood crosses over into disease and catches the pilot light of anxiety. All of a sudden a fire burns up in my mind. I have gotten good at keeping my outsides stoic when I am struggling, but my insides feel like quicksand. My nerves and my sense of reality will reduce to ashes before I can catch hold of them.

+ + +

I am sitting across the playground from my oldest while she plays. I keep my distance because I know it's good for her. If I were closer, I would help her too much and make her doubt her own ability to climb. So I let my worries eat away at me over here in private, under the tree.

It seems so loud out here, like the volume of nature is on full blast. I am excruciatingly conscious. I know just how far my little one has to crawl out of the shade before the concrete will burn her hands and knees. I know there is an ant pile under the bushes near the bike rack. The lack of control I have makes me feel nauseous. I am sure the other parents can see right through me. They probably think I am hovering. I worry about their eyes on me.

My daughter slips and falls through the bars of the ladder. Instantly, I envision her with a cracked skull, blood all over, brain swelling. I race over to her, but she runs right along as if nothing ever happened.

Because the fears in my head are not real.

This is always how it goes, though. I cannot help but to sift through every hypothetical scenario in my mind trying to find imaginary danger.

My baby will be burrowed into me nursing, quiet and full of peace, but all I can see are fictional bruises all over her body. At bath time, I see both of my kids drowning, flailing in terror, when really they are splashing each other and their laughs are echoing off porcelain walls. Whenever we leave the comfort of our home, I am sure I will accidentally leave them in the scalding car, and their organs will boil in their tiny bodies. Whenever I am alone, I am panicky, first thinking I have forgotten them somewhere. That nightmare haunts me even when I am sleeping.

These sick thoughts harass me whenever there is a breach of confidence. Everything is always turning into monsters.

I fight anxiety every day. The fact that it never thoroughly dissipates makes me feel like a failure; but I am not a failure. For the first time in my life I have something louder, something bigger than anxious whispers and heckling panic. And that something is the love I have for my children.

Although my brain might be incapable of functioning perfectly, my heart isn't. My heart is healthy, flawless, and strong. My heart is what fills my babies' bellies, what tucks them safely into bed, and makes sure they breathe all throughout the night. My love for them is what gets me out of bed when the earth is too alive, and it is what hushes the demons when I lie in bed at night. This love loosens the grip on my lungs and reconnects my nerves to my bones. The strength of my heart makes up for where my mental health lacks.

So I will keep fighting their monsters, and I will continue to fight mine; because they are my voice of reason—no match for any demon—and I am their warrior.

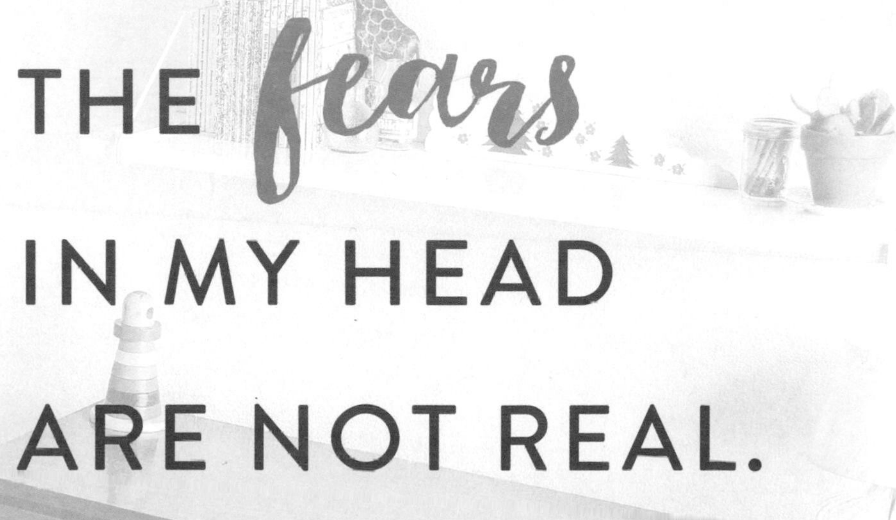
THE *fears*
IN MY HEAD
ARE NOT REAL.

27

A LOT OF BOTH

by Elena Krause

I was five when I found out my brother was different. A friend told me. Different from what? I didn't know. Different from my friend, for sure. Different from me? I didn't know that either. Was I different, also? Were we both different?

The friend was at my house, and we were in the backyard, carving an extravagant castle from a mound of muddy sand.

"Somebody should teach TJ how to speak English," she said as she used a neon pink shovel to dig out a moat for the perimeter. She said it like it was nothing, like she was casually dropping a piano on my head from a ten-story building.

What a weird thing to say, I thought as the heavy sentence landed. My brother *did* speak English. We had the same parents, and they both spoke English too. Two years my elder, he'd been there for every minute of my life thus far. He was my best friend. If he couldn't speak English, I'd know that.

Still, something about this comment felt valid even in its absurdity. People often asked me what TJ wanted, what he'd just said, how he felt, what he was doing. From the time I learned to form sentences, I'd talked for both of us. I'd been his interpreter, and I'd never questioned it until now. But really: why would anyone need me to translate English to English?

My friend went into our house to find my mom and let her know about the oversight, and I followed, reeling. I think I expected my mom to set the record straight. Maybe I thought she'd get mad and tell the kid, "No, *you're* the one who needs to learn to speak English."

But my mom wasn't surprised or angry. She thought it was funny. "Oh, he speaks English," she laughed. She was probably baking bread or mopping the floor at the time, brushing her bangs away from her face with the back of her hand. I can't remember exactly what she told the kid, but it had something to do with the fact that my brother had Down syndrome, and that the Down syndrome made it hard for him to speak clearly. Yes, it maybe even sounded like he was speaking a different language.

I was shocked.

I mean, the first part didn't surprise me at all; I *knew* what he had. I could've told anyone that. It was this thing that people said about him, like it summed him up. But it meant virtually

THAT WAS
THE DAY I
LEARNED MY
BROTHER WAS
different.

{ BE YOU }

nothing to me at that age. It was just part of his introduction. *This is TJ. He wears glasses and has blond hair and Down syndrome.* Maybe I thought the Down syndrome had something to do with glasses. A fancy word for bad vision? I wanted glasses too, desperately, but my eyesight was perfect.

That second part though: *difficult to speak clearly?*

It had never occurred to me. We spent so much time together that communication came easy. Kids need that stuff pointed out to them, I guess.

So that was the day I learned my brother was different. That was also the day I watched my mom tell someone else he was different, watched her smile and laugh and explain without a trace of discomfort or sadness. It was soothing to me, the way she spoke about my brother, the way she named his difference in the same voice she used to say normal, easy words, like *hello* and *good-bye*. I wonder now how long it took her to get to that place.

Did she know then that I'd be taking my cues from her? That the way she spoke about my brother's disabilities would shape the way I saw anyone with disabilities from there on in? That conversation demonstrated that TJ's differences were not something to be ignored or belittled, but they also weren't something to focus on and make a big deal about. They were, and that was all.

In the same way, that day was a big deal—and it wasn't. Life carried on and nothing changed. It was TJ, my best friend and me, his interpreter.

When I was eight, a different friend asked me another heavy

question. It was recess, a clear and blindingly white winter day, and my classmates and I were building igloos, chopping out chunks of frozen snow to use as bricks. As we chipped and hacked and dug and stacked, one of the girls glanced over at my brother, right in the thick of the building project with the rest of us.

"Hey," she said suddenly. "Do you think they'll ever invent a cure for what TJ has?"

That question, innocent enough, and maybe even meant to be hopeful, bothered me immensely. For years.

I know that for a lot of people, Down syndrome is a disorder, a diagnosis, a life sentence. I know now that my mom cried when she found out, though I didn't understand *why* for a long time. But for me, his little sister, it was just a part of who he was. I had a shaky understanding of what makes a person who he or she is, but I felt sure, even at such a young age, that his so-called disorder was a building block at the very base of him, that it was woven right into him on purpose, a thread that connected everything to everything. I was sure that if someone tried to pull that string, he'd just come apart. He wouldn't be the same person.

From that day forward, I had dreams about pills and needles and doctors, about mom taking him to the hospital and him coming home "cured." In the dreams, I wouldn't recognize him. He'd be taller and his face would be thinner and his eyes would be wider and his fingers would be longer and more capable. His tongue would be smaller, and he'd talk the way I did; he wouldn't need an interpreter. He'd walk in the door, and I'd go to hug him, and he'd treat me the way my best friend's older brother treated her. He'd say, "Elena, you're so annoying. Go away."

I'd wake up crying and feeling guilty. Shouldn't that dream be a happy one? If this thing, this Down syndrome, *was* such an affliction, shouldn't I want him to get better? Was it unloving of me to wish this on him just because I wanted things to stay the way they were? Did I really want him to have to live at home for the rest of his life, never marry, never have kids? Did I want that for my parents?

I struggled with that.

I've never really stopped struggling with it. I struggled with it when a friend announced that their baby would be born with that extra chromosome. I struggled with it when my own doctor informed me that my risk of having a child with Down syndrome was high because of its frequency in my family history. I struggle because, to me, Down syndrome isn't a scary, foreign thing. It's a distinct and beautiful characteristic of someone I love. And I struggle because I know how it changes the quality of living for the person affected and for his or her caregivers. It comes with other health challenges, sometimes mobility challenges, sometimes extensive hospital stays, surgeries, appointments, heart conditions, thyroid conditions, and so on. Sometimes a life is shorter for it. How could I wish for it, or wish it on anyone? And on the other hand, how could I ever wish for a world without TJ and people like him?

It's *hard*, but it's not just hard. It's beautiful, but it's not just beautiful. It's a lot of both.

But I really do believe that TJ, exactly as he is, is the way he is for a purpose. I believe that about everybody, so why wouldn't I believe that about him?

To me, everything about him is so intentional and so good. I have seen his effect on the lives of other people in our community, on the other kids at school, on my parents. And mostly, I've seen the effect he's had on me. This is absolute and undeniable.

And that's what I always wish I could communicate to women who are googling those two words for the first time after a mind-numbing, world-flipping doctor appointment. That's what I had to remind myself when I thought about the possibility that my own son might have all of those mannerisms and characteristics my brother has. *This child is going to be exactly who he is, and it's not going to be an accident. It's going to be hard and it's going to be beautiful, no matter how many chromosomes he's born with. He's going to teach me a lot of things, and I'm going to be better for knowing him—exactly the way he is.*

28

THE INVISIBLE THREAD

by Anna Quinlan

My youngest son did not grow in my womb, but in my heart. While his older brother stretched my body in every direction with fifty pounds of pregnancy weight, our youngest grew in another mother's belly—a mother who was unable to care for him and safely surrendered him at the hospital. But at the same time, he also miraculously grew inside my body as well. Not physically, of course, but I felt his presence palpably and mysteriously before I ever laid eyes on him, a tugging on the invisible thread that will connect our hearts forever.

We started the adoption process with a sense of purpose and excitement. We attended an orientation meeting in a nondescript county government building, finally bringing to life an idea that we'd been discussing for years. As the necessary classes, paperwork, and background checks ensued over the following months, some of that excitement waned a bit, quieted by the noise of all the to-do lists and logistics.

Four months into the foster-adoption licensing process, just before Christmas, my excitement disappeared entirely. My heart felt heavy inside my chest, crushed under the knowledge of how the foster system works, and the fact that it has to exist at all.

I couldn't stop thinking about the mother who would birth my baby. I wondered if she was feeling the same things I felt when I had been pregnant the previous year—overwhelming love, excited anticipation, the promise to be a good mom. Did she rub her belly every morning as she woke up, grateful to feel her baby kicking around in there? Did she look at other babies and wonder what her baby would look like? Did tears come to her eyes like they did to mine when she thought about finally feeling that baby resting on her chest?

I hoped all of those things were true. But knowing what would happen next, that a Child Protection Services worker would have to take that baby away from her due to "abuse or neglect," my heart broke for her. There are a million roads that could have led her to that end—addiction, mental illness, an abusive partner, failure to impart basic life skills—but no matter what the circumstances were, I couldn't fathom a situation in which having your baby taken away from you is not completely devastating. My heart broke for her.

My heart broke for the baby too. He would become a part of

our family only after the most primal relationship a person can have was irreparably broken, and then he'd grow up without a biological family. In so many ways, it felt downright unnatural. In so many ways, it seemed impossible to survive.

I confessed my heartbreak to a friend who was an adoptive mother herself, hoping for reassurance that it wouldn't feel like this forever, that my heavy heart wasn't a sign that I wasn't ready for this. She listened intently. And then, when I expected her to offer comfort and reassurance, she simply told me to write down the date. She explained that on the road to adoption, overwhelming emotions sometimes correlate with important events in the life of the child, only to be realized after the adoption. It seemed a little far-fetched to me, but I was desperate to do something, anything, with my heartbreak, so I made a quick journal entry and hoped it meant something.

My heartbreak eventually passed, and life carried on. There was more paperwork, more meetings with social workers, and life as usual for our family of three.

And then, on an ordinary October day, our social worker called. She told us the facts: There was a newborn baby boy in the NICU. He had been born prematurely to a mother who was unable to care for him, and he needed parents to call his own. It was the news we had been waiting for, praying for, hoping for.

I was devastated.

I was devastated to know that he was alone, and had been for the first two weeks of his life. I was devastated to know that he would never know his biological mother, or anyone who shared his DNA, for that matter. I was overcome with sorrow for him.

HOME
SWEET
HOME

We met him the next day at the hospital, and the weight of his four-pound body in my arms was the only salve that could have possibly begun to mend my broken heart. He was perfect. He was ours. His heart was connected to mine, and I could feel it as surely as I'd felt anything in my life.

My friend called. "What was the date?" she asked. "What was the date that your heart was feeling so heavy last year?"

I didn't have to look at the journal entry. It was late December, the twinkling Christmas tree had felt like an anemic symbol of joy along the treacherous path I was walking. I didn't have to consult a calendar to see the miracle, to do the math. Nine months after that period of heartbreak, my son would be born.

My voice quivered on the phone. "Nine months," I whispered.

"Nine months," she said. And then, the truth I had longed for all along, the most comforting thing I had ever heard in my life: "He was never alone. He was always in your heart."

What does it mean to be a family? What does it mean in our family, with one child who grew in my womb and another who grew in my heart?

"There is an invisible thread that connects our hearts together forever," I say. I tell my two boys that it can stretch all the way to the sky and there is no force great enough to break it. This is what it means to be a family, I tell them. We are connected forever. No matter what, I will never stop loving them.

My boys are three and five years old now, and they are

mostly fascinated by the science-fiction nature of this invisible thread. They want to know what would happen if it were struck by a ninja sword, or if one of us learned how to fly far away, or if someone was killed by a bad guy. "What would happen to the invisible thread then, Mom?!" they ask excitedly, hoping to have finally stumped me.

My answer is always the same: "The thread that connects my heart to yours will never, ever break, no matter what, and it will connect our hearts together forever and ever. That's what it means to be a family." They are unimpressed with this answer. Bored, even. They want fireworks, a battle, a catchphrase worthy of a spandex-clad superhero. And while parenting young children certainly has plenty of firework moments, the invisible thread metaphor is meaningful precisely because it is steadfast to the point of boredom, consistent to the point of predictability.

There is an invisible thread that connects our hearts together forever.

In all of the mundane, everyday tasks of motherhood, my ultimate goal is to show them again and again that I will always be here for them. I will never let them go hungry. I will never let their stories go unheard. I will never let their wounds go untended. I will never stop pulling them close. I will never stop being their mom.

Even though they roll their eyes at me, it's good for me to say it out loud. Not just to reinforce the idea for them, but to remind myself too. It's good to remember the foreverness of motherhood, to imagine them as awkward elementary schoolers and then moody teenagers and someday, distant college students who don't call home nearly often enough. There is comfort in knowing how many opportunities I'll have to show them that I'm serious about this invisible thread—that I will love them as best I can no matter what, until the end of time.

29

RECKLESS

by April Hoss

It's hard to be pregnant again after a loss. It feels a little like being in a campy horror film. You know right away which character is doomed, which doors should stay locked, which scenes mean it's all over. You want to scream at the TV (or in the shower or the car . . . lots of screaming seems appropriate), but you also know screaming would be futile. In fact, that should be the title of this bloody, predictable film you're living in—*Futile*.

I was innocently sitting at Starbucks, editing a synopsis due to an editor, weighing the pros and cons of pulling the trigger on the chocolate croissant that had been eyeballing me, and then the next sip of my coffee tasted funny. Off somehow. The certainty of it struck me there in my seat. Not because it was planned or any effort had been made or because of anything to do with dates and temperatures. I just knew. I packed up my laptop and notes, drove home, walked straight to the bathroom, did my thing, found my husband and son in the living room and announced flatly, "Well, I'm pregnant."

I did not feel excited. I did not feel emotional or ecstatic. I felt meh. *Oh. Fine.*

We went out for nachos, a preplanned lunch date, and I heartlessly pushed my chips around the plate. My husband and I did not hold hands and trade baby names; we didn't look across the table teary-eyed and talk about the beautiful miracle happening in our midst. I'm not sure what he did. I stared out the window until our food was cold.

(As an aside, had I realized I'd soon be saying farewell to all food, I would have made a smarter choice that afternoon. While we're on the topic, I'd like to now apologize to cheeseburgers, Caesar salad, and the entire canon of Mexican food. When we at last reunite, it will be Shakespearean.)

I didn't plan to tell anyone. All the emotional heavy lifting required when announcing a miscarriage far outweighs any excitement at the initial belief that a baby is coming. But the morning sickness I didn't expect led to a prolonged absence from basically my entire life. My new exile to the couch meant there would be no guarding this pregnancy or the inevitable tragedy that would ensue. We told people. And again and again, friends and family said the words I didn't feel: "That's so exciting! Congratulations!"

Are you congratulating me on my broken belly with the abysmal track record, on the unfortunate baby taking up residence there, or on my "bad luck" diagnosis of two years ago? I thought every one of these things. What I said was, "Thank you."

When it comes to being pregnant, I will always sleep believing there is a monster breathing under my bed. I will never post a photo to social media holding a pregnancy test as the color gives way to great news. I won't download pregnancy trackers or start a newborn board on Pinterest. I will Google though. Boy, will I ever. The web's siren call of statistics and forum discussions waiting to tell me either all is well or all is lost is undeniable. I will hunch over my phone, thumbs ablaze, going insane.

Mania will take hold.

I hire a doula and then immediately regret the decision. I draft in my head the cancellation e-mail I'll have to send in a week or two.

I take my son to a baby store, and we choose two newborn outfits that look mostly gender neutral. I don't remove the tags.

I text some girlfriends, asking for prayer because I am pretty sure I am having a miscarriage due to my sudden ability to eat lunch. I tell my mom the same thing. No one thinks lunch is all that frightening. I creep back to my forums.

My husband asks if he can share the news with his coworkers. I bite my lip. Doesn't he know they'll all pity him?

I watch my son push his wagon around the yard and hear him say one of the three phrases he's mastered, "OhboyOhboyOhboy," and feel relief that this loss will go over his head. He looks back at me, his only companion for 85 percent of his days, and I feel guilty that he won't have a brother or sister to play with soon.

At my lowest, I begin composing a Facebook post to inform our friends and family that the pregnancy they'd been rooting for is over. Admittedly, I do this while eating ice chips and saltines, laid up like a wounded zombie. In the midst of my madness, I never actually present any symptoms of miscarriage. I present symptoms of hopelessness. I just can't name it.

A new worry sets in as I write this sad status update. What if people don't believe that a person can have three consecutive miscarriages and still love God? I have to be very strategic in my spiritual PR. God is counting on me to defend Him.

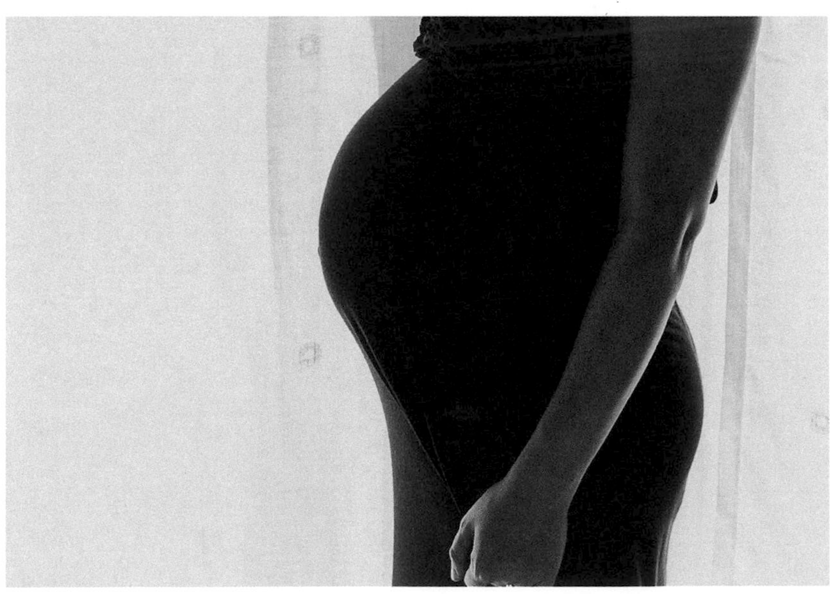

I never could get that status update just right.

Somewhere in those days that felt like one unending hangover . . . with the flu . . . with mono . . . with military-grade food poisoning, my husband asked if I loved this baby, the one I was waiting on to die.

"No." My chin quivered. "I don't want to. This one will just leave me at the altar like all the others. Seems reckless to start loving it."

He thought for a moment, his blue eyes wandering to our fireplace and blocks and Thomas the Train books scattered on the floor. "Don't you know all love is reckless?"

Even in the worst horror films, there is a turning point: the main character at last sees the roommate/girlfriend/camp counselor for who they are and starts running out of the monster-infested woods.

"Don't you know all love is reckless?"

Help my hopelessness, my unbelief.

At my husband's words, I turned my feet away from my woods.

All love *is* reckless. I know this. My mind understands that age or disease or accident will come for us all. I'm going to die, but that doesn't keep me from loving my parents or my brother or my friends or my husband and son.

But with this baby, I was letting death win. I insisted that this love be safe. I demanded that this love be sterilized. Sterile things are cold, empty, hard. I felt like I couldn't love this baby because I was hurt by my history, but let's be real: I couldn't love this baby because I was afraid.

Forget that.

There's a story in the Bible that used to mean very little to me, a horror story in its own right. A desperate father seeks out Jesus to heal his demon-possessed son. The demon was especially strong and had been tormenting this man's boy for years. He wanted his boy healed, but life without this demon seemed unimaginable. Like all my favorite people, this man was very honest with Jesus. He uses the phrase "If You can," in his request. He tells Jesus, "I believe. Help my unbelief."

I can't read this story anymore without weeping. That is the song my cold, hard, frightened heart is singing as it thaws back to life. That is my battle cry for my baby. Help my hopelessness, my unbelief.

God, keep this tiny heart beating.

God, give me a reckless heart.

30

THE PACIFIC

by N'tima Preusser

2007

Almost a decade ago, I saw you for the first time. We were floating on a sultry rock halfway between the North Pacific Ocean and the East China Sea. You were across a spacious, squeaky high school lunchroom in Okinawa. Your eyes were bright green, foreign yet comfortable. You wore a band T-shirt snug across your chest and a studded belt loose around your hips.

I had such a crush on you.

Our paths were parallel until, all of a sudden, they weren't.

Our friendship was composed of awkward hallway high fives, until we spent our first evening together under that big oak tree in our neighborhood. Remember that night? We talked for as long as our curfews would allow. We were wrapped in thick, humid heat, fireflies landing on our knees, and we were the only two people on the planet. Our love was slow and then rapid. I was dizzy. I was only fifteen, but what I felt for you was all-consuming. It was as palpable as the moisture that sat in the air.

There wasn't a question. You were it.

We spent the next fifty days falling into one another. And then my family had to move away. California was so far from Japan. Our faces became pixels, our voices became waves, our words resided on paper. It hurt to be away from you, but love filled the distance.

2011

There was white lace in my dress and a pink bouquet in my hands. You were wearing a nice vest and a Lego tie pin. We were summer babies being wed in a blizzard; white powder fell in our hair. We were eager to begin a life together. It was easy to get used to sharing a roof and four walls and a mattress and laundry. We had waited our whole lives for it. We had waited our whole lives to exist together, without endless water between us.

2013

Your cells are dividing inside of me. Our DNA swims together inside our first daughter. A baby being hand sewn inside of my swollen womb.

We brought her into the world with an August sunrise through trauma, an ungodly amount of blood loss, and a resuscitated heartbeat. Grief and displaced fear caused depression to crash in without warning. The water that used to hold us on opposite ends of the earth now sits above us, and I can't breathe. Like a baptism we didn't consent to, the water of new life washed away all that we had ever known. We did our best to not let the salt water permeate our marriage. You traced my stretch marks like they were trophies. You looked into my eyes and found substance in the emptiness on my face. You held on until my brain wasn't sick. Your love was big enough to bring me back to the surface.

2016

Today, I am on the floor with a babbling, fussy seven-month-old and a vibrant, argumentative two-year-old. I am a human jungle gym and teething toy. You walk through the door after a day at work and you are tackled by little limbs as toddler laughter fills our entryway. Our eyes meet, and it's sitting between us again. One hundred eighty-seven quintillion gallons of water. The Pacific.

Our children are the Pacific Ocean.

But this distance between us cannot be bridged easily. These children are real and their needs are pressing. They are humans who need to be nursed, bathed, rocked to sleep. They are crying in the night for us and begging to be on our hips every waking hour of the day. Physical contact between you and me is usually sandwiched between our daughters. Conversations revolve around their existence. Their noise is shouting from every direction. When the moon and the sun are constantly pulling us in separate directions, the tide is begging to break.

I'm chopping onions for dinner. You didn't eat vegetables when we first met, but you do now. You come behind me and wrap yourself around my waist. The kids are both demanding our attention, but all I notice is you. We laugh at the tears coming from my face and I say something stupid and I kiss you. I feel fifteen again. Dizzy. Beautiful. Loved.

I have such a crush on you.

By the end of the day, we are just two teenagers crazy about each other. To an outsider it looks like Netflix and ice cream and flirting and my legs seat-belted across your lap, but there's so much to say about the significance of what's there. These moments with you are what fills my body with oxygen again.

The girl that I was before all of this is kept alive by my love for you. I see her in my baby-bearing hips and in my sunken eyes. I see that broken child, once blanketed by insecurities, with a solid spine now, and a voice she isn't afraid of.

This water has shaped you and me; it has molded us, created something that the girl I used to be and the woman I am now is so proud to be a part of, together.

Because that's what water does (if you stand firm enough to let it).

At the end of this ride together, I imagine what we have left will resemble the Grand Canyon. They will refer to our love like a magnificent landmark. A piece of history. We will have built something that represents our beautiful life together. The view will be unimaginable. All because we chose to run with the current, together. Never sitting still. And our children will know that our love never diluted, or disintegrated, or divided.

Because love always filled the distance.

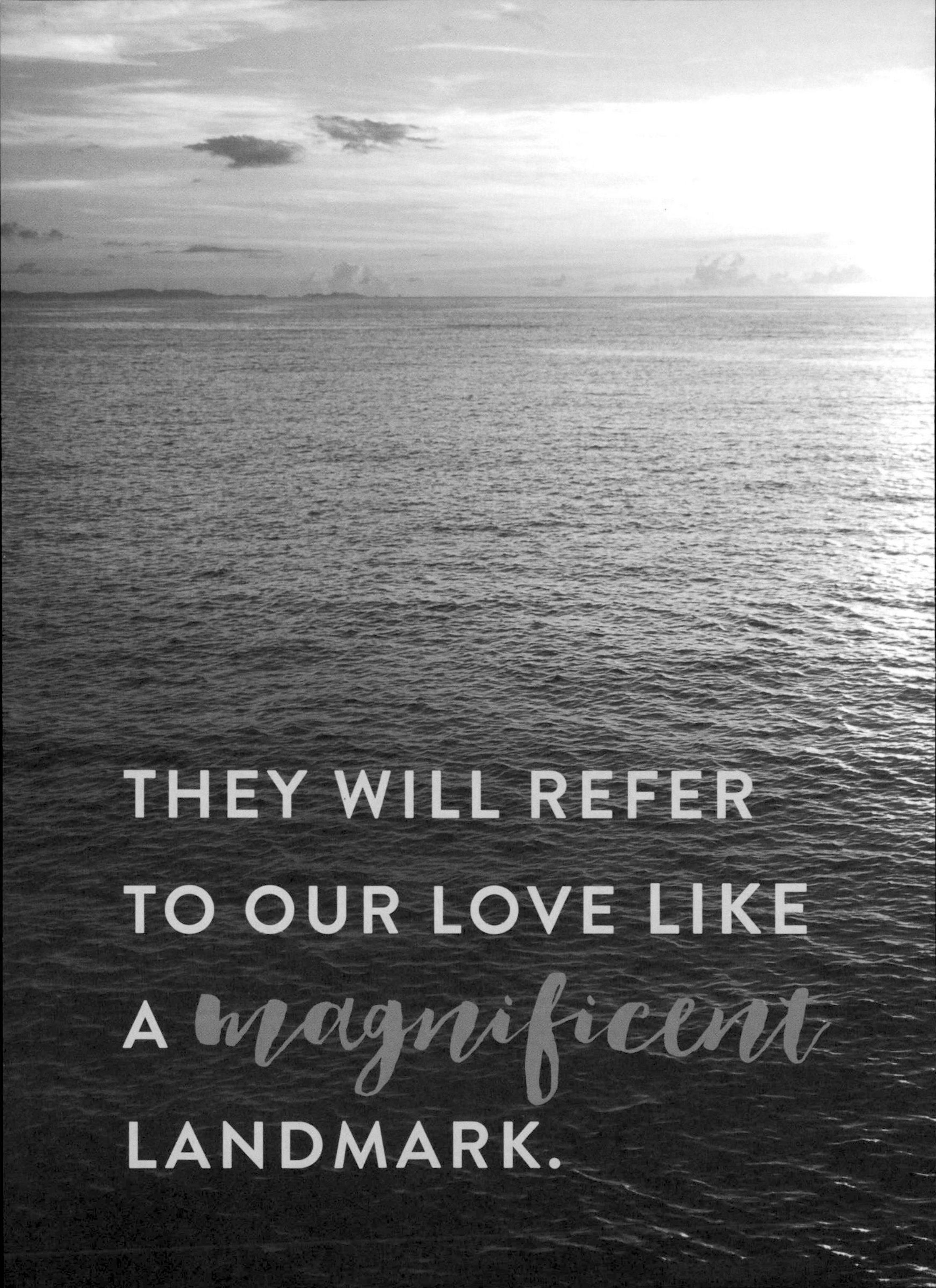

THEY WILL REFER
TO OUR LOVE LIKE
A *magnificent*
LANDMARK.

31

MY BODY IS YOURS

by Melanie Dale

I should've listened to my husband. I should've locked the door. But I never want my kids to feel like they can't get to me when they need me. Still, I should've listened. As I stepped out of the shower, my daughter burst into the bathroom to tell me something, and upon realizing that I was buck naked, promptly forgot what she was going to ask and stared wide-eyed at my pasty body.

"Um, hello? Please leave," I commanded resignedly. She jumped back to reality from wherever her brain was orbiting, shook her head, mumbled "Sorry" and ran out of the room. I thought that was the end of it, but later that evening, I overheard her describing my nether parts to her siblings. "You guys, Mom has hair *down there*!"

Rather than be adult about it and let it go, I decided to up the ante. "That's true! And you will too!"

My kids started screaming in horror, "*Why?!*"

"It's called *puberty*," I explained. "When you get older, extra hair will suddenly sprout from your privates and armpits. You won't see it coming. Just, *poof*! One day, everything will change."

This is how I handled it. I'm not saying I handled it well. Oogedy boogedy puberty is going to sneak up and get you in your sleep one night while you're lying there helplessly in your *Beauty and the Beast* nightgown.

One of my kids is on high alert for these changes, making me inspect armpits for possible hair growth. What an honor to have my face that close into an armpit at the end of a long day of jumping on the trampoline. I feel like puberty must be close based on the fresh aroma wafting through the air. *Deodorant, baby. Discover It.* This child is excited and anticipating the momentous change, although I've told her to please enjoy her remaining hairless time on earth because she'll spend the next fifty or sixty years trying every new product on the market to remove said hair.

What is it about motherhood that is so grounded in our physical bodies? It is so corporeal, and there's no room for squeamishness or prudishness. Our kids are all up in our humanity. I've never been through labor, or much of a third trimester, but even with two-thirds of a pregnancy and the two adoptions that I've experienced, motherhood has been firmly rooted in my body.

WHAT IS IT ABOUT
MOTHERHOOD THAT
IS SO GROUNDED IN
OUR *physical*
BODIES?

When I was pregnant with my son, I experienced morning sickness in the evening. Someone had warned me that morning sickness was really all-day sickness, and sure enough, every night around *CSI* o'clock, my stomach roiled, and not just from the entrails strewn across the TV screen. Every evening, I found myself dry heaving over the kitchen sink, suspended in a permanent state of seasickness. Eventually, sometime during the second trimester, it abated, save for the lingering motion sickness that still plagues me to this day whenever I try to ride a spinning ride or swing on a swing. When I learned I couldn't have more babies in my belly, I made the reasonable assumption that this would also mean no more morning sickness. But that turned out to be false.

During my first trip to Ethiopia to adopt my daughter, we ate pounds of Ethiopian food, shoveling the delicious *injera* and *wat* into our mouths. I loved Ethiopian food and couldn't get enough of it. One night we met friends at a restaurant known to cater to expats, a Westernized establishment where I ordered something that looked like a bean chimichanga. This was where we went wrong. We should've stuck to eating Ethiopian food in Ethiopia. A chimichanga had no business in the Horn of Africa. Over the next few hours, I began to sense a disturbance in the force. My stomach seemed to double in size, and I barely made it back to the room where we were staying before I began a back-and-forth dance of hovering one end of my body or the other over the toilet in our bathroom.

The contractions didn't stop until my body had expelled every. Last. Bean.

But that was just a fluke. I joked that the Chimichanga Incident was my adoption morning sickness, but didn't give it much thought until I was standing on another continent, preparing to adopt another child. A couple years later, near the end of our three-week stay in Latvia, I started to use up the food that had accumulated in our mini-fridge in the apartment overlooking the picturesque church in Old Riga. I slathered what was left of the delicious goat cheese on crackers and thought about our final trip to court the next day, more than a two-hour drive away on snowy roads.

After tucking our newest and oldest child in bed, I felt a familiar cramping and grabbed a bowl from the kitchen before running into the bathroom. *The goat cheese must've gone bad.* I groaned into the stainless steel bowl as I began a night of turning inside out. Knowing my daughter needed her sleep, I tried to moan quietly and wondered at the human body. If we're 60 percent liquid, then I'd say 59 percent of it came out of me in that cozy apartment that night. The next morning, I slid into the car to make the trek across country to the little courtroom, a shell of a human being, swearing off goat cheese forever. My new daughter looked at me quizzically, and I reassured her that it wasn't her; it was the mini-fridge.

Three different continents, three different stories . . . same stomach. I experienced the morning sickness rite of passage—the nausea of impending motherhood—in the most well-rounded way possible.

At our town's annual Fourth of July parade, my preemie son nursed hungrily underneath the Hooter Hider. He was tongue-tied, and breastfeeding was a challenge, but one he had risen to handily. Sweat trickled down my sides in the sweltering Georgia heat as the high school band marched past us. I worried that my baby must be as hot as I was, trying to eat his second breakfast of the morning. As the decorated floats rolled by, my son had finally had enough, and grabbing the fabric panel with his sweaty fist, he yanked it out of the way as the man sitting next to me leaned over to make small talk. I was torn between embarrassment at my exposed breasts and triumph that I'm a nursing mom of a son who should be able to eat with a cool breeze against his little face. My nipples experienced their own freedom that Independence Day.

I didn't nurse my other two, but that didn't stop us from experiencing unexpected exposure. Children always find a way. Standing in the church lobby one day, my two-year-old daughter clung to me, still not used to all the faces and chaos of her new life out of the group home. Desperately trying to regulate her stressed-out body, she grabbed me by the knees and shoved her head back and forth through my legs. She got into her new

> **My daughter enthusiastically grabbed my skirt and lifted it over her head like a parachute, exposing my underwear to the world.**

game, in and out, back and forth between new Mommy's knees, and smiled as my skirt covered her head. I planted my feet and tried to stay upright while my husband talked on and on with people in the lobby. I made a mental note to come up with a code word for "Get me out of here!" because he was not picking up on the intense laser-beam eyes I was shooting his way. Just as I had had enough, my daughter enthusiastically grabbed my skirt and lifted it over her head like a parachute, exposing my underwear to the world, and as I hastily shoved my skirt down against my legs, I worried about the state of affairs under there. I'm not sure there is a readiness level for that kind of exposure in church.

A few years later, when our oldest visited us for the first time, we took her to our neighborhood pool. We had just moved in a couple weeks earlier, so I was trying to meet people and make friends. She jumped in, the too-loose swimsuit bottoms nearly falling right off her tiny bottom as she hit the water's surface. She shrieked with laughter and began jabbering in Russian. Her chaperone explained that she'd never been in a swimming pool before. I jumped in with her and began tossing her through the air into the water again and again. I was Supermom. I was amazing. *Watch me, neighbors, as I show you how amazing I am.* After probably the thirtieth time hoisting her through the air, I looked down with horror to discover that my nipple had worked itself loose from my bandeau top and was waving hi to my new neighbors. *Watch me, neighbors, as I show you how amazing I am.* The man I'd spoken with when we entered was staring intently at the wooden fence around the pool. We'd just moved in two weeks earlier, and I wondered if we would need to move again. At least our stuff was still in boxes. *Most new moms slip a nip during nursing*, I thought. I'm a new mom to an eight-year-old, but still that thing popped right out.

I guess no matter how we arrive at motherhood, we end up sick and naked a lot of the time.

Yesterday, one of my daughters wiggled her grubby fingers up into my armpit out of the blue. Startled, I jumped and exclaimed, "No! Please don't ever touch my armpit!"

"Mommy? Did you get rid of the puberty?" she asked innocently, "Girls don't want the puberty to show?"

I answered, laughing, "Yes, in our culture women usually shave the hair off our armpits."

I think about the puberty and how the puberty leads to motherhood . . . eventually . . . way in the future. Way, way, way. And when motherhood comes, everything changes. When we become mothers, our bodies cease to be just ours. *Hey kids, my body is yours*. And then over time, we slowly get it back. We finish morning sickness, we deliver and eventually wean the baby, we set the child down to walk on her own, and finally, with sweet relief, we lock the bathroom door.

32

IT'S THEIR DAY TOO

by Katie Blackburn

I'm certain this story is familiar to you: one child wakes up much earlier than she should, another one sleeps longer, and the third is a newborn, so all bets on sleep are off already. Forget being at the park on time, because older sister just squeezed her whole fruit pouch on the carpet. The gas tank was empty when you got in the car, and now you're coasting. Grocery shopping gets abandoned on the way home because the baby is screaming—and enduring that volume a moment longer than you need to is simply not an option. Naptime is thrown off completely when you cannot sync their schedules, and just as you get one lunch cleaned up, the other one wants to nurse.

YOU'LL BE TEMPTED TO CALL IT WASTED.

But it's their day too.

All of a sudden it is 3:30 p.m, and you have not answered a single e-mail. One load of laundry sits ready to be folded in the dryer, the other load washed and wet but probably needs a re-wash because it was left there overnight. Dinner is spaghetti and a jar of sauce you had in the closet; it's the absolute best you can do tonight because you never actually made it to the grocery store. You hand the toddler another applesauce pouch and pretend it's a vegetable. Nothing got tidied up today, and no one's bed is made. There were three episodes of *Dora*, though, and there would have been a fourth if Dad had not gotten home in time to come in as relief. It's just been *a day*.

The crazy, unpredictable, frustrating days usually come when we have the most to do, don't they? Kids have a sixth sense for this kind of thing. Have a deadline to meet? Your kids are likely to cry for the thirty minutes you thought you could sneak in some work. Is there a meeting or class to prep for? They will not sleep at the same time for one minute that day (even though their naps always overlap by at least an hour). The baby will want to be held more some days; the toddlers will need more refereeing on others. Then you'll get crabby because your day went nothing like you planned, and you'll be tempted to call it wasted.

But it's their day too. And when you think about it, they had a pretty good one.

Big sister learned how to clean up the messes we make. After the fruit-pouch incident, when she saw me with the stain remover and a towel, she brought over a baby wipe to help. She watched, and she learned something.

The baby was cared for. Our little ones need lots of touch to know they are safe and loved. I gave that affirmation in bulk today, and he felt it.

And together these little children watched their mom handle stress, but very imperfectly, so they also watched me apologize when I took that stress out on their dad. They saw me whip together a meal for our family, and I know the kids did not care one bit that our dinner wasn't gourmet. I never got to my e-mail, but I did read them a book, blow bubbles, and catch flying toddlers at the bottom of the slide.

I did not check off many to-do boxes today, but my little

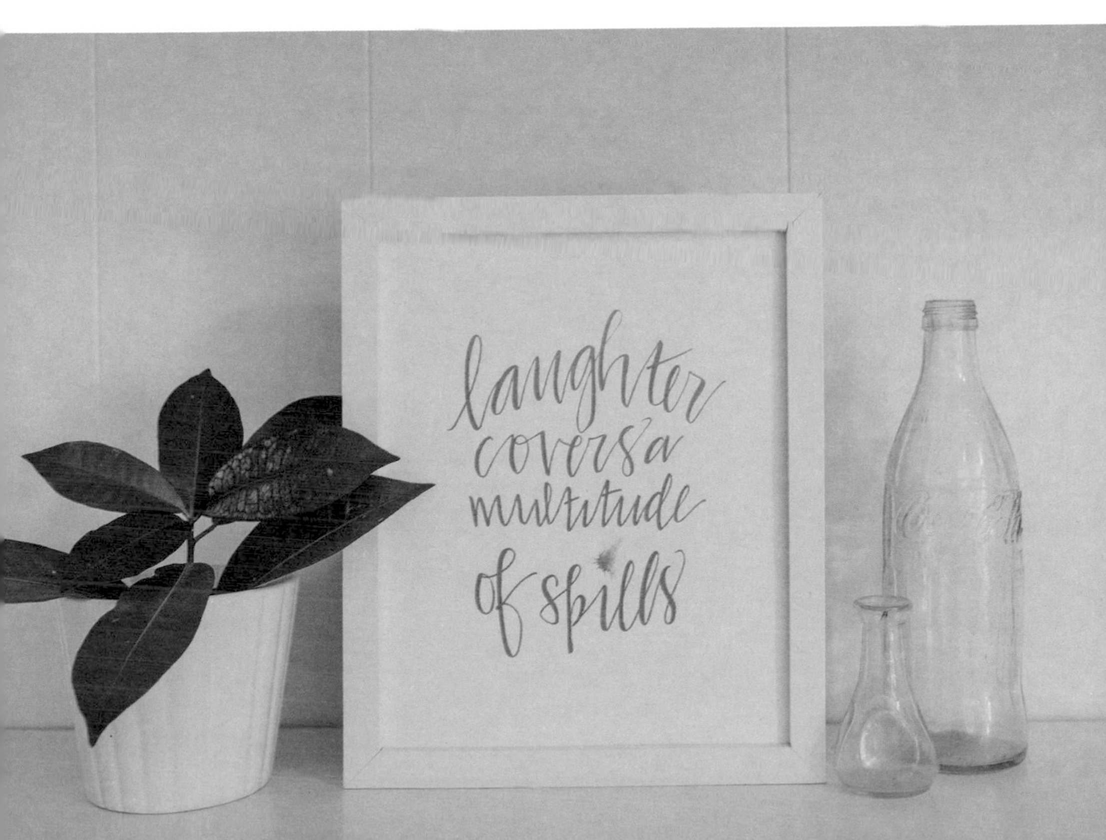

ones did: learn, play, eat, sleep, read, and repeat. And I helped them do those things. If I measure each day by *my* list, the days are not always very good, but when I look at each day like it is their day too, because it *is* their day, well, then most days are better. A lot better.

That's where I want to land at the end of every day: assessing it by what we learned and how often we laughed and the new words we heard. For us mothers, the word *productivity* needs a different connotation. The measurement of success needs different metrics, ones that include diaper changes and dishes, teachable moments and affirming hugs. I've come to accept that at the end of the day, it is okay that I was not a good writer / small business owner / teacher / (insert role here) today. But dang, I kept three kids under the age of three alive and fed. We played and talked about trees and chased after bubbles in the breeze. All of them are sleeping safely in their beds tonight. And that made today a pretty good day.

33

THIS TIME AROUND

by Lesley Miller

This time around I feel you early, fifteen weeks, tapping on my insides and making yourself known. There is no denying you're a baby, low and hidden in my body, a secret hello that only I recognize. It will be weeks before anyone else can feel you, and I soak up the intimacy of it being us. Just momma. Just son.

With you I experience no morning sickness. I am so thankful for this reprieve because your darling-but-demanding siblings need me every day starting at 7:00 a.m. I wait for my usual first trimester stomach pains to kick in, but they don't arrive either. The fast food cravings do, and I know better than to deny you a Jack in the Box taco or a greasy In-N-Out burger at 11:00 p.m.

The cravings will stop eventually, and I'm a happier person when I'm not hungry. Just typical first trimester stuff.

Instead, I embrace my growing belly with no attempts to hide my pregnancy from the world. My stomach muscles, once firm and tight, expand early to make way for you. I have no choice but to pull the bag of faded maternity clothes out from under my bed for one final round. There is a belly band or two in the stash, and I think about how eager I was to wear them with your sister. *See? See, world? I'm with child! I am part of the club!*

This time around, I know that a rubber band is much more effective in extending my jeans a few more weeks, but simply embracing those comfy maternity pants is an even better option.

I pay more attention this time, and I'm surprised to find that even though I've done this before, it's all still delightfully mysterious. How do you fit in there? Is that an elbow or a knee? Will you be born with just a little bit of hair, like your sister, or a lot, like your brother? No one else knows your movements like I do, but only God knows what you look like and who you will become.

The weeks pass and we tell your older brother and sister about your impending arrival. They are thrilled, and curious, and perhaps even mildly confused. There is arguing at the breakfast table about whether you will be a boy or a girl, and then tears when we tell your sister that you are, in fact, a growing ball of testosterone.

And with the knowledge of your sex, we move into the name discussion. It's a swift conversation really—there's only one left on the list that we can agree upon—and we don't overanalyze. Neither of us will have our first choice name, but we know that a lot of things in marriage and parenting are compromises. The most important thing you should know is that you were never a compromise. You've been longed for and waited for and loved since before you were even conceived.

Just like the last two times, we hold your name secret for the growing months. The only people who know are the mailman and the woman who gives me a pedicure. *Luke*, I whisper when they ask. Occasionally I want to hear your name out loud, and it thrills me each time because it reminds me you are more than tiny movements and doctor appointments and sciatic pain.

This time around, I know that every pound gained, every ligament stretched, is bringing me closer to meeting you.

I view your growth like training for a marathon—I might look weak and slow, but I feel strong because of the bigger purpose: you are being created by the same God who created me. I revel in my womanhood, staring at my curves in the mirror, fascinated by what my normally boyish physique can do instead of willing for it to all be over. I snap photos—not for Instagram, but for my own memories—because I want to remember the days when my body was a home for someone so important.

Last Saturday your daddy set up the crib in fifteen minutes flat. There was no fanfare or frustration, besides some annoyance at your brother, who insisted on "helping." I did not take photos for the baby book. Over the years your sweet dad has set the crib up over and over and over again, with every move and every room transition. He can change diapers and swaddle babies with the same speed, confidence, and precision as crib assembly, and I know that someday he'll pass along these skills to you.

YOUR LIFE IS *delicate* AND *precious*, SOMETHING I WILL NEVER TAKE FOR GRANTED EVEN THOUGH I'VE DONE THIS BEFORE.

This time around, I'm a lot more confident too. I receive less advice from strangers, perhaps because they think I know what I'm doing by now, but more likely because I'm too busy wrangling your siblings out of the shopping cart to make chitchat.

When those strangers do speak up, usually to tell me I look awfully big for being thirty weeks pregnant, I'm not offended. Because *I am big*. I tell them, with pride, that I grow beautifully large and healthy babies. "My last one was nine and a half pounds," I say. I don't worry much about your weight or mine. At the doctor's office I've learned to never look at the scale. It doesn't matter, because it all works out in the end. Really, it does. It will take me a year to lose the baby weight, and my body is never going to look like it did when I was twenty-eight. But I also know that you won't be a baby forever. There will be time to run and lift weights and practice yoga again in the future.

Instead, in the meantime, I will responsibly put my black yoga pants where they belong—in my hospital bag. They are the same ones I've worn after every birth because they are dark and stretchy and hide blood. They hold all the pads up where they're supposed to be, and are somewhat slimming—two very important considerations in postpartum fashion. I'll pull them out of my bag a few hours after you arrive because my bulleted birth plan no longer includes a line requesting that I deliver in my own clothes. In fact, my bulleted birth plan no longer exists. You, baby, will have a mind of your own. I've learned this the hard way.

This time around, if I want an epidural, and I most certainly do, we'll leave for the hospital sooner.

When you come out, I hope they can hand you to me right away so I can kiss your sticky, bloody head and stare into your puffy eyes, and whisper, "You're okay; I'm here. You're okay; I'm here," just like I said to your sister and brother. These words always feel right in the first panicked-but-peaceful moments of new life. I lay awake in the final weeks of pregnancy, worried that we won't have those moments together, because I better understand all the things that can go right, and all the things that can go wrong. Your life is delicate and precious, something I will never take for granted even though I've done this before.

This time around—this third time, this remarkable time, this fleeting time, this never-ending time—it is also, probably, the last time. And so I will slow down. I will revel in the firsts of the lasts. I will remind myself that the newborn days are long and tiring, and then they are over. I will remember that the pain is temporary and to hold you close and often.

While your birth will not make me a mother for the first time, you are making me a mother all over again. You are reminding me of how far I've come, and how far I still have to go; how ready I am and also how much I need a Helper. You are a familiar mystery, a tiny piece of God. I will both know you and be known by you, while also spending my whole life trying to understand you better. I may know how to birth and breastfeed and burp you, but I still have so much to learn about how to mother you. And I can't wait for the honor of fulfilling such a mighty task. Because you, my child, are a sacred gift that will only come around this time around.

ABOUT COFFEE + CRUMBS

We are mothers and storytellers. Plain and simple. We believe that the very essence of motherhood can be found in the sweet spot between coffee and crumbs—in that magical place between calm and chaos, beauty and mess, joy and sacrifice.

Coffee + Crumbs launched as a collaborative blog on July 1, 2014, and had 2.8 million pageviews in the first eight weeks after three of our posts went viral. We struck a chord with mothers all over the world and have been gratefully writing for them ever since.

Today, Coffee + Crumbs is a beautiful online journal filled with hundreds of stories about motherhood, love, and the good kind of heartache. Our website has become a safe haven for confessions and truth-telling, a place where mothers can sigh in relief and say, "Me too."

Visit www.coffeeandcrumbs.net to learn more.